JOHN ESTEN COOKE, VIRGINIAN

JOHN ESTEN COOKE, VIRGINIAN

BY

JOHN O. BEATY, Ph.D.

PROFESSOR OF ENGLISH IN SOUTHERN METHODIST UNIVERSITY

KENNIKAT PRESS
Port Washington, New York

JOHN ESTEN COOKE, VIRGINIAN

TO

C. ALPHONSO SMITH

PREFACE

AMONG Virginia writers whose careers have come to a close, John Esten Cooke holds a conspicuous place. He is by far the most voluminous, and has exerted great influence on later novelists. He is thoroughly Virginian, and is perhaps second to Poe in the intrinsic importance of his work.

Since neither Cooke nor his literary background has been the subject of a definitive study, I have, in writing this critical biography, relied very slightly on printed sources but am in consequence largely indebted to a number of Virginians and others who have helped me gain access to first-hand material. Dr. Robert P. P. Cooke and Mrs. Charles Lee, children of the novelist, have kindly placed at my disposal eight manuscript volumes and hundreds of letters and other papers which belonged to their father. Cooke's nieces, Miss Mariah Pendleton Duval and Mrs. Carter H. Harrison, have likewise furnished me with manuscripts and have entertained and instructed me with reminiscences of their uncle. My research work has been facilitated by the courtesy of the officials of the Library of Congress, of the New York Public Library, and of the Library of Columbia University. I owe much, for assistance of one kind or another, to each of the following gentlemen: Mr. J. B. Ficklin, Jr., the Southern genealogist; General Thomas T. Munford, a boyhood and Civil War friend of Cooke; Reverend C. Braxton Bryan, Cooke's pastor in the eighties; Professor Killis Campbell; Mr. W. G. Stanard, Librarian of the Virginia Historical Society; Mr. H. R. McIl-

PREFACE

waine, Librarian of the State of Virginia; Dr. Oral S. Coad; Dr. R. F. Dibble; Professor Jay B. Hubbell, whose forthcoming *Virginia Life in Fiction* will serve as an excellent background to this biography; Dr. Carl Van Doren, Literary Editor of *The Nation*; Professor George Philip Krapp; and Professor William Peterfield Trent, the leading historian of American literature. My wife, Josephine Powell Beaty, has given me some very valuable criticism and has helped prepare the manuscript for the press. To Mrs. Beaty and to Messrs. Coad, Van Doren, Hubbell, and Trent my indebtedness is particularly great.

J. O. B.

CONTENTS

CHAPTER I

JOHN ESTEN COOKE, VIRGINIAN

John Esten Cooke, Virginian

CHAPTER I

EARLY LIFE—CHOOSING A PROFESSION

AT the age of twenty-one John Esten Cooke composed and copied in a ledger an account of his early life. Like all of its author's note-books and diaries, this autobiographical fragment was written in a readily legible hand which on the title page and at chapter headings is even comparable to engraved lettering. The beautiful manuscript is further embellished with three-color pen and ink drawings of childhood scenes. "I was born," the future novelist and historian recorded in his initial sentence, "in the house on 'Ambler's Hill,' Winchester, November 3, 1830." Delightful as this sketch is, it does not lend itself well to copious quotation. It is not only rambling, but is heavily weighted with the moral platitudes of a serious-minded youth. Cooke, moreover, with typical self-effacement, did not make himself quite sufficiently the central figure of his narrative; he spoke nearly as freely of his relatives as of himself. That he was not writing with an eye on the possible general reader of the future is, however, shown by the fact that he omitted—merely because they were obvious to him—such important items as the names of his parents. Throughout his life Cooke was, for his environment, very democratic—far more so than his brother Philip, who wrote of the glory of "caste;" but it is nevertheless surprising that a Virginian should begin any life history without some attention to ancestry. Whatever the youthful Cooke may have thought of his forebears—whether he merely took them for granted or considered the question unimportant—many of them had graced an honorable birth with lives of service and achievement.

According to one of Cooke's diaries, an ancestor of the name came to America from the county of Hereford, England. The date of his arrival is not recorded, but he must have been an early settler; for a descendant, Nathaniel, great-grandfather of the novelist, was a native of Boston. Nathaniel Cooke seems to have moved later to Philadelphia, where, according to the novelist, he became a wealthy ship-owner and assisted the Colonial government with his money.

Nathaniel's son Stephen Cooke, as so many of his descendants were destined to do, led a life which was both successful and romantic. He is variously said to have attended Princeton and to have been sent to ''one of the English universities;'' in any case he became a physician. He saw service in the Revolutionary War as a surgeon, and was in Fort Moultrie when the British attacked it. From Charleston he set out by sea for Philadelphia, but was captured and carried to Bermuda. Here the authorities seem to have allowed him the freedom of the island, for he was soon well acquainted with the ''staunch Whig,'' John Esten, a prominent government official who was at one time president of the Bermuda Assembly. Stephen fell in love with Catherine Esten, daughter of John Esten and grand-daughter, on her mother's side, of Nathaniel Spofforth, a gentleman, of Yorkshire origin, then prominent in Bermuda. Before the end of hostilities, the young surgeon appeared in Boston, presumably through an exchange of prisoners, and shortly served his country in a new capacity by bringing salt from the Bahamas in "an old shackly schooner." When the war was over he returned at once to Bermuda. Here he married Miss Esten and for a time made his home, but he subsequently transferred his practice to Turk Island in the Bahamas. In 1791 he moved to the United States, settling in Alexandria, Virginia, where he acquired considerable property. He established himself in 1801 on an estate in Loudon County and died fifteen years later, long survived by his British wife who lived to be revered by numerous grandchildren.

Fourteen children[1] are said to have been born to Stephen and Catherine Esten Cooke. Of this numerous family two sons, the eldest and the youngest, attained to a degree of nation-wide importance; while another, the third in order of birth, was a prominent Virginia lawyer who became the father of the novelist.

Stephen's eldest son was named in honor of his maternal grandfather. His name, John Esten Cooke, has frequently been confused with that of his better known nephew—the more easily because the uncle was also a writer. The elder John Esten Cooke was born in Boston on March 2, 1783, on a visit of his parents to that city. Having received the degree of Doctor of Medicine from the University of Pennsylvania, he began his practice in Warrenton, Fauquier County, Virginia. He removed in 1821 to Winchester where his writings on fever, pathology, and therapeutics began to attract attention. In 1827 he was elected to the "Chair of the Theory and Practice of Medicine in the University of Transylvania," and took up his new duties in Lexington, Kentucky. With the collaboration of Dr. Charles W. Short, he

[1] Notes on six sons and two daughters, together with many other genealogical details pertaining to seven generations of the Cooke family, are found in the series, *Notable Southern Families*, published in *The Lookout* (Chattanooga, Tenn.).

founded, in 1828, the *Transylvania Journal of Medicine and the Associate Sciences.* Becoming more interested in theology than in medicine, Dr. Cooke took part in a religious controversy, put himself through a severe regimen which even included bleeding—intended to keep his brain clear—and produced in a very short time a book, *The Invalidity of Presbyterian Ordination.* He was soon made "Professor of the History and Polity of the Church" in the newly established Episcopalian Seminary at Lexington. Later, when Episcopalianism waned in Kentucky, Dr. Cooke became a professor in the medical institute at Louisville. From this position he retired to a farm on the Ohio, where he died in his seventy-first year on October 19, 1853.

Stephen's youngest son, Philip St. George Cooke (1809-1895) was born in Virginia. He was graduated from the United States Military Academy in 1827, served with distinction in the Mexican and Indian campaigns, and was a brigadier-general in the Union forces in the Civil War. In spite of his career as a most active soldier chiefly engaged in frontier work, General Cooke found time to cultivate his share of the family bent for writing. From his pen came several volumes, of which the most important are perhaps *Scenes and Adventures in the Army: or Romance of Military Life,* which was brought out by Lindsay and Blakiston at Philadelphia in 1856, and *The Conquest of New Mexico and California; a Historical and Personal Narrative,* published by G. P. Putnam's Sons in 1878. While in the West the young officer wrote industriously to his older brother, the father of the novelist, sought the aid of the nephew in arranging the publication of articles, and in other ways made a rather notable effort to keep in touch with the Virginia members of his family. His different environment, however, furthered the development of political ideals which threw him against his relatives in the

Civil War, thus adding an interesting page to the family history.

John Rogers Cooke, third son of Stephen and father of the novelist, was born in Bermuda in 1788. He came to America with his parents, attended William and Mary College and Princeton, studied law, and settled for practice at Martinsburg, (now) West Virginia. He served in the War of 1812, and in the Virginia legislature, but the crowning achievement of his career was his work with Madison, Marshall, and others in 1829 in drafting the new constitution of his adopted state.

According to his son's negro mammy, John Rogers Cooke was the glass of fashion of the scarcely more than border town of Martinsburg. He was soon in love with Maria Pendleton, a daughter of Philip Pendleton of Berkeley County. If the young lawyer had actually had in mind the supplementing of the literary talent of his future children, he could not have more wisely chosen his wife. Miss Pendleton, a grandniece of "the well-known Judge Edmund Pendleton of the Revolution," was a member of a talented family. John Pendleton Kennedy, the author of *Swallow Barn* and *Horseshoe Robinson*, and David Strother, who is perhaps better known under his pseudonym, "Porte Crayon," both had Pendleton blood in their veins. As Stephen Cooke did not know the Pendleton family, his son sent him a picture of Maria, and wrote for permission to ask her in marriage. Almost immediately, however, in a second letter he announced his engagement. To the first letter the old gentleman replied that, if the portrait was a good likeness, he and his wife "would not have any objection;" he insisted, nevertheless, that it "would not be prudent" to become involved "in the expenses of a family" before enough had been saved for at least one year of possible misfortune. After receiving the son's second letter, however, the father naturally felt that the seeking of parental approval had been "a mere compliment;" consequently he concluded: "All that is now necessary for us is to express our sincere wish that Heaven may bless you, and that you may be happy in the choice you have made." Upon acquaintance Stephen came to value his daughter-in-law highly. His appraisal of her picture may be taken as evidence of her personal charm, and her correspondence shows her to have been a worthy and capable woman. When the pressure of law practice detained her husband in Charles Town she herself oversaw the work on "Glengary," the Pendleton estate to which they had moved from Winchester. She recommended that he "try to get home before dark on Sat'y," described interestingly the garden and lawn improvements, and told of having the servants work where each would be most "efficient." In addition to intellect, charm, and house-wifely skill, Mrs. Cooke possessed another admirable quality, a deep affection for her family. The novelist's first memories are of the "bright and beautiful" mother who watched over him in childhood. "Dear little John Ety is my shadow," she wrote to her husband in the spring of 1833. "I have just put him to bed in my room and he is as happy as possible."

John Rogers Cooke and his wife had thirteen children, of whom five lived long enough to figure prominently in family papers and letters and to leave descendants. The five, in the order of birth, were Philip Pendleton, Henry Pendleton, John Esten, Mary Pendleton, and Sarah Dandridge. Of the remaining children Anne (the oldest daughter), Edmund Pendleton, and Edward St. George ("Sainty") reached adolescence. One of the sons who died early had borne the name John Esten before it was given to the future novelist.

The early childhood of John Esten Cooke differed little

from that of the normal ante-bellum Virginia boy brought up on a country estate. Of the four brothers he mentions in his autobiography, Philip and Edmund were too old and Edward was too young for intimate companionship, but John records that he and Henry prowled about together "in the run, over the woods, up the trees, doing all manner of mischievous things." In retrospect he seemed to have been a "far more important personage" then than as a young lawyer and author in Richmond. "A merry child, also a great pet, on a farm is a miniature king. Thus Henry and myself . . . wandered over the domains of Glengary at our own will and pleasure." The two boys flew kites, fought bumble-bees with shingles, hunted hickory-nuts, ate melons and peaches "gathered by stealth," and fished "with pinhooks for minnows." John had the farm-boy's sense of proprietorship, for he speaks of "swearing lustily" at the town-boy apple-robbers who descended upon the "Glengary" orchard. He performed various little tasks from gathering strawberries to watering horses, and went through the usual blundering but instructive attempts at service; one day, for instance, he "went to burn stumps with Henry and set the whole field on fire." "Put me," he wrote in the autobiographical sketch, "in the middle of negro boys and girls, with a whip, a top, a torn straw-hat, and wagon: freckled and barefooted, and my portrait in those times is complete."

The most fascinating figure with whom John Esten came into contact in his boyhood was his eldest brother, Philip Pendleton Cooke, who was fourteen years his senior. Philip was perhaps the most brilliant member ever born in his family. At fifteen he entered Princeton, the alma mater of several of his ancestors, developed a fondness for Chaucer and Spenser, and received 'his baptism of print in the *Knickerbocker Magazine*. He contributed to the first vol-

ume of the *Southern Literary Messenger,* and at his death
in January, 1850, left unfinished in this magazine a story,
The Chevalier Merlin. Philip's only volume, *Froissart Ballads, and Other Poems* (Carey and Hart, Philadelphia,
1847), showed him to be a master of verse technique. One
of the poems, "Florence Vane," seems sure of immortality
in American anthologies:

> "I loved thee long and dearly,
>   Florence Vane;
> My life's bright dream and early,
>   Hath come again;
> I renew in my fond vision
>   My heart's dear pain,
> My hope, and thy derision,
>   Florence Vane.
>
>   .   .   .   .
>
> "Thou wast lovelier than the roses
>   In their prime;
> Thy voice excelled the closes
>   Of sweetest rhyme;
> Thy heart was as a river
>   Without a main.
> Would I had loved thee never,
>   Florence Vane!
>
>   .   .   .   .
>
> "The lilies of the valley
>   By young graves weep,
> The pansies love to dally
>   Where maidens sleep;
> May their bloom, in beauty vying,
>   Never wane
> Where thine earthly part is lying,
>   Florence Vane!"

The ballads show greater talent than does "Florence Vane,"
but, because of their length and the less universal appeal
of their subject, are not as well known as they deserve
to be.

The tragedy of Philip Pendleton Cooke's life is revealed in the numerous still extant letters which he wrote to his father. It has been said that when he was not hunting he divided his time between law and literature. Hunting and literature surely kept him from making a success of law, just as hunting and law prevented him from fulfilling his true destiny as a poet. A harassing result of the forfeited profession or the betrayed talent was a lack of funds which was practically unrelieved except by gifts from his father. But the Philip of his brother's autobiography—described as reading, writing, and storing his hunting trophies in the detached son's-house or "office" typical of Southern estates—had not yet entered upon his brilliant troubled years. He was, nevertheless, already contributing to magazines, and John Esten, nourishing an undeveloped literary talent, was doubtless duly impressed. The "noble voice and dark eyes" as well as the "delicate black mustache" of the poet were vividly recalled many years later. To Henry and John, however, Phil's crowning attribute was his skill as a hunter, and the scent of gunpowder almost invariably accompanies the poet into the pages of his brother's autobiography, whether he has killed a deer "at eighty yards with a ball under the eye," has brought in an unusually fine wild turkey or Indian hen, or has merely exploded a large fire-cracker in a manner calculated to impress a small boy. The death of a favorite dog was the occasion of a burial in state with a cortège of small brothers and negroes, the poet firing a salute over the grave of the "pointer-emperor." Before little John was strong enough to raise his gun, Phil would hold it and allow him to pull the trigger, but in spite of, or perhaps because of, this early experience John never developed a fondness for hunting. Poetry and the chase can, however, scarcely have completely dominated Phil's early life, since, at the age of twenty, two years after leaving Princeton, he married Miss Willie Anne Burwell, who came to live at "Glengary." "Sister Willie," as she was henceforth to be known to the large family of marriage kin, was to John a "being come from fairyland." She must have been gratified by her reception in her new home, for the family letters in the next quarter of a century speak of her in terms of the deepest affection.

The Cookes at "Glengary" were, as has been suggested, a mutually devoted family, and were not averse to expressing their feelings. Scores of letters, by words as well as by the reflection of generous actions, bear testimony to their affection for each other. John never tired of paying tribute to his mother, but his subsequent extreme devotion to his father was slower in developing. "Pa" at this period was a "dignified and most affectionate being of superior nature to the rest of the world who gave me all I wished or capriced . . . and never thwarted my desires." As may be surmised, the boy's love was not confined to relatives; the family slaves shared largely in his good-will. Upon one occasion an obstreperous negro youth named Sawney had been sold to a "gentleman in Winchester who engaged never to sell him to the South." John went up to the sobbing slave-mother, Mammy Giddy, and told her "not to cry," that he "would be her son." From that time the black woman loved him "especially and particularly," and forty years later, a decade after the war, was the nurse of his children. "God forbid," he wrote toward the end of his life, "that I should ever be anything but proud of that old negro's affection. Not so long as I live."

It is not surprising that a boy capable of such deep affection should have soon exhibited a reflective turn of mind. "Sister Willie says I was a bright, sunny-faced child, full of mischief, with dancing eyes, round red cheeks, and very gay; yet spite of all often sunk in deep reveries. I would sit, she says, at a table with an open book before me, one arm round the book, my head supported by the other hand, pretending to read, but really in profound thought.'' At seven, swinging on the garden gate, the boy first realized that ''all was imperfect.'' He recalled ''looking at the hearse on grandma's death with an unbelieving, unrealizing simple curiosity.'' He believed firmly in ''certain country-side superstitions of the period,'' and would hasten by a closet on the stairway where a ''white-lady ghost'' resided. A feeling of anything but interest was excited in him by the ''girls from town'' who came out to play with his sisters, Sal and Mary; but he approved of his cousin ''Puss'' Kennedy, whom he regarded vaguely as a sweetheart though he had never seen her—''like the minstrel Rudel, who never *saw* the dame of Tripoli.'' When ''Glengary'' was destroyed by fire, the family moved temporarily to the overseer's quarters. Although forbidden to go near the ruins, John did so surreptitiously to collect nails from the ashes, and ''became more serious in the presence of those old tottering walls of the burnt house, through whose window-openings poured sun, moon, and the white dim starlight.''

The destruction of ''Glengary'' and its furnishings perhaps dictated in large degree the removal of the parents in the summer of 1838 with their eight children to Charles Town, where the father's office was situated. On the farm Henry and John were already accustomed to being summoned by the farm bell from work or play to read a *History of Scotland* or Charles Rollin's *Ancient History*, and at Charles Town they were entered at the school of a Mr. Sanburn—perhaps the original of Parson Tag of *The Virginia Comedians*—a ''most severe and unconscionable old rascal'' who was obsequious to parents but fell into ''diabolical rages'' against his pupils. Outside of this school, which John bitterly hated, his life was little different from what it had been in the country, except that white boys succeeded the black ones as companions. The prowling now, save for Saturday rambles, was largely confined to the various quarters of the town. John participated in the usual ''harum-scarum youthful deviltry,'' broke a window, paid frequent visits to the livery stable and the town pump, played ball, and exchanged green pears for powder through the garden fence with a town rowdy between whom and himself ''there was an uninterrupted contest as to which should bully the other—the great world in miniature!'' While one of his small friends was trying to make an electrical machine, and another was championing a circulating library, John was on the one hand profoundly impressed by the new railroad, and on the other was already peopling old houses with the figures of romance. The history read at ''Glengary'' gave place now to the *Tales of a Grandfather*, which he read aloud to an aunt. The reading still seems to have been rather compulsory, but in view of the boy's future work it was surely seminal. This round of life in Charles Town was soon to be interrupted. A fast increasing reputation as a lawyer and the problem of educating his large family determined John Rogers Cooke to remove to Richmond.

The country he was leaving was one of the most remarkable spots in what was then perhaps the most romantic of the American states. Immigration and nature had combined to make the region unique. In Clarke and Frederick, and the two adjoining counties now in the Eastern panhandle of West Virginia, the German civilization of Pennsylvania stood face to face with the English civilization of Virginia. The Germans were the first to come in numbers and pushed southward up the fertile valley; but Lord Fairfax was no less desirous of securing and extending his vast estate, and actually built Greenway Court to the west of the Blue Ridge. Many families from Tidewater joined him and even today his old neighborhood, the present county of Clarke, partakes of the nature of an East Virginia colony. Since the Scotch-Irish had already been disputing the Valley with the Germans, there were to be met daily in Winchester, Charles Town, and Martinsburg three distinct races, all of which are portrayed in Cooke's romances dealing with the Valley of Virginia. In the days before railroads the Potomac was one of the great highways to the West. Interesting travelers were constantly passing. Cultured families were found in the river counties, while the old border still survived in portions of the Alleghanies. A stage trip to some of the more mountainous counties would discover cabins where lived men to whom, a few decades before, an Indian raid was not a rarity. Cooke's first book, *Leather Stocking and Silk*, derived its title from this contrast as did a later, *The Last of the Foresters*. Lying as it does between the Blue Ridge and the Eastern Alleghanies, the Valley of Virginia affords a variety of beautiful scenery. The sun rises as well as sets over a fine chain of mountains. Unusual features in the landscape result from the calcareous nature of the region. The bee-hive cave in *Fairfax* is surpassed by the actual caverns of Luray. Numerous ponds and sink-holes mark the fallen roofs of smaller caves. The scenery probably did not appreciably affect John when he lived in the Valley, but he must have been impressed in retrospect when, in his new home, his excursions and visits took him along the banks of the James, through the swampy territory of the Chickahominy, or elsewhere in the Tidewater region.

The Cookes arrived in Richmond in March, 1840, and "lived first in the house below the Capitol Square—one of the brick dwellings built by Vial and rented at an enor-

mous price.'' John Rogers Cooke's service as a member
of the legislature and of the state constitutional convention
of 1829 had already made him a circle of friends in Richmond, and his family was hospitably received in that city.
The centralization of American intellectual life around New
York had not then begun, nor had the New England literary
coterie yet risen to overshadowing fame. Boston, New
York, Philadelphia, Baltimore, Richmond, and Charleston
were centers of local culture; and of these cities Richmond
was perhaps not the least important. It possessed a much
larger relative population than does the Richmond of today
and was the capital of a state which extended to the Ohio
River. Unfortunately lacking a university, Richmond was
nevertheless in close touch with the venerable College of
William and Mary and with the newer University of Virginia, the number of whose students was greatly increased
by the development of sectional ill-will, with the consequent
dislike of Southern fathers to send their sons to the Northern universities. The city was also visited by the great
actors of the time and sustained several publications, among
which was the *Southern Literary Messenger*, the most
notable magazine that has yet appeared in the South.

John Esten's sudden change from the border to the capital resulted in a marked intellectual stimulus. He no
longer needed a bell to summon him to his books. The
''harum - scarum'' became an alert, ambitious student.
''George and myself were soon sent to the Academy,'' he
writes. ''I remember distinctly our début there—dressed
in black cloth from head to foot, with white straw hats, and
in profound amazement.'' The day of his entering this
school saw the beginning of the most intimate friendship
of the first half of Cooke's life. Benjamin Watkins Leigh,
Junior,—a son of an associate of John Esten's father in
drafting the State Constitution—refused the invitation of

one Richard Heath to "pitch into the little stranger," engaged him on the contrary in conversation, liked him, and made his path easy. The autobiography refers meagerly and in the most general terms to this period, but Cooke attended Dr. Burke's school as well as the Richmond Academy. He set down accounts of rambles in the neighboring woods, and of swimming trips to the falls of the James, a picturesque place soon to be invaded by factories, much to the chagrin of the Richmond schoolboys. Weighty problems were discussed in boyish letters, and quarrels were adjusted in the most solemn fashion. Though all the boys in this group practiced target-shooting, there is no evidence that they ever regarded their skill as a means of composing their differences. John Esten evidently no longer considered girls as disagreeable as he once found the "little maidens" of the Valley, now considered "nice" in retrospect; for in writing his recollections he recalled "so vividly . . . that star" of his "youth or rather childhood with her long dark curls and tender smile and musical laugh."

Whatever the school-boys of this period may have done occasionally, they apparently found their greatest interest in literary societies. Oratory was the forte of the men of the old South and it was natural that their sons should emulate them. Cooke carefully preserved the "Records of the Proceedings of the Franklin Debating Society" for 1845 and 1846. This society met first at Burke's School and later at the Academy. Its sessions were usually held twice a week and at least once on successive days. Young "Wattie" Leigh stood out as the leader among his friends. After serving twice as president he refused reelection, but later on heeded the call to a third term in order to save the organization which his successor had nearly shipwrecked. Young Cooke had taken part in several debates, usually on the justification of certain famous executions in history or on the relative merits of certain pairs of virtues, and had won as a rule except when pitted against "Wattie." He had been defeated for a minor office. His hour of triumph came, however, in a manner that reflects credit on the critical acumen of his fellow members. An essay was read once a month, and John Esten made so favorable an impression with his that it was "resolved that the society keep Mr. Cooke's essay." Election of officers came next on the order of procedure, and Cooke received a landslide. Perhaps the outgoing president wanted to take a last good-natured thrust at the future chairman; perhaps John Esten was feeling a bit reckless because of his new honor; at any rate in the remainder of the session, as is solemnly recorded in the minutes, "Mr. J. E. Cooke was fined 12½ cents (once for disturbing the society 6¼ cents and again for interrupting Mr. Munford 6¼ cents)"—as many penalties in an hour, it seems, as he had hitherto received in his entire membership. Cooke's administration was successful and he was reelected. When a member resigned "on account of the president's arbitrary administration of justice," the society accepted the resignation and sustained the chair by a unanimous decision. Cooke secured the passage of a by-law providing "that if any member run or move faster than a walk in the room where the society is holding its meetings he shall be fined 6¼ cents." The usual hour of gathering was four or five o'clock in the afternoon, but the protracted nature of some of the sessions is shown by the requirement (established in a season of long days) that each member bring a "whole candle" on the first meeting of each month. In an unguarded moment the society changed its name to the "Skull and Bones" and spent several dollars in having an anatomical device engraved with the constitution upon parchment. The inappropriateness of the new name soon became apparent, and on the first occasion of John's presiding the "S and B" was ordered stricken out and Franklin restored. This society touched the outside world in maintaining friendly relations with at least one similar organization, and in having men of prominence as honorary members.

John Esten's success in the literary society would naturally have suggested a career as a lawyer. Of the Southern Democrats recently prominent in national affairs, many are products of these forensic training camps. Oscar Underwood, John Sharp Williams, and Woodrow Wilson—the latter a medalist—were, to mention but one organization in one school, nearly contemporary members of the Jefferson Society of the University of Virginia. But apart from the influence of tradition it is not surprising that a boy of 1845 should have looked to law as an attractive vocation. Before the great modern era of business and engineering, men of local fame, especially in the eyes of the young or the not particularly well informed, were, in times of peace, almost always holders of public office. Law in 1845 was of course almost a prerequisite to statecraft, and though Virginia was becoming less important politically by the mid-century, the profession still retained its attractiveness. Furthermore, John Esten's family environment pointed toward law. He revered his lawyer-father, some of whose pronouncements on topics of the day he recorded in his diaries. His brother Philip, ostensibly a lawyer, was unsuccessful in Virginia, but, in writing to his father, was the architect of air castles in which he figured as a senator from Missouri. John Esten Cooke, at approximately the age of sixteen, thus began the reading of law under the guidance of his father. Consideration was given to the desirability of his going at once to the University of Virginia, but it was decided that he had best pursue his study privately in order that, when he did matriculate, he might graduate in one session. The youth set his heart on entering the law school in the fall of 1847, and in August wrote accordingly to his father, who was then in the western part of the state on a trip combining business with recuperation. The letter caused the absent parent much worry, for it found him financially unable to provide for a step he greatly approved.

From an early age John Rogers Cooke exhibited a lack of business foresight perhaps surprising in one of his ability. His lavish use of his means may be illustrated by his treatment of poachers at "Glengary"; he objected strongly to their presence, but once they were on his estate he would send out to them trays of ham, bread, and wine. In the middle forties his younger children were reaching the expensive age. Moreover his oldest son now had an increasing family and was only in part self-supporting. Cooke's father had thus been, in spite of his large fees, heavily involved in debts by the combination of Richmond life, numerous dependents, and reckless generosity. On the fifth of September he answered his son's letter, stating the lack of funds but expressing the hope that a matriculation a few weeks later might be arranged for. "I will send you to the University *as soon as possible*. Go you shall if God spares my life and health." John did not go and two years later almost to a day wrote a similar letter in reference to the session of 1849-50. His private study had been dragging rather slowly through the two years, but he was now hard at work on his books in eager anticipation of entering the University. "You seem to have commenced the good work," the father replied, "and I devotedly hope that you will not fall back into idleness, light reading, and frivolous *associations*." The son was reminded that a knowledge of law remained while summer friends were ephemeral, and was promised "that nothing but the *ascertained impossibility* of raising the money" should prevent his being entered at Charlottesville *"on* or soon *after,* the first of October." This plan likewise fell through, and John evidently determined to consider college no more. When the family exchequer became able again to stand the drain, he withdrew his claim in favor of his younger brother Edward. Thus ended his dream of becoming a University man.

The father's reference to John's frivolous procedure was apparently the unjustified utterance of an aging man forgetful of his own youth. The "idleness" consisted in attending speeches, concerts, plays, and everything of an intellectual nature that came to Richmond; in keeping informed on the politics and literature of the day; and in frequenting the social gatherings of young men and women of his own years and station in life. In a diary minutely recording the doings of this year, no entry was made which revealed the slightest trace of unbecoming or improper conduct. On the other hand, it would seem only natural that the constant holding up before his eyes and sudden withdrawal of his cherished desire for a higher education should have engendered a certain lack of application.

Cooke had, however, another excuse. The "light reading" was Carlyle, Tennyson, Irving, Emerson, Dumas, and a score of others in English, American, and French literature—names which are today the classics of those who are condemning "light reading" still. In fact, the youth was careful in his reading, made notes on it, imitated it; was seriously beset, withal, by the desire of becoming a man of letters. At a very early age he had written an unpreserved piece, "The Well of St. Kean," which he always regarded as his first original literary work. Cooke was a great lover of autumn; he was "disposed to imagine" that his character resembled that "fine and beautiful season, so dreamy, full of memories, so warm and cool by turns," and his second com-

position was "some lines on Autumn which Pa liked." The
year 1849 is very fully recorded in a ledger which combines
the features of a journal and a commonplace-book, and reveals, much better than his earliest published articles, the
state of mind of the writer. In this ledger were copied numerous original poems, as well as imitations of Poe's "To
One in Paradise," and of several of Tennyson's poems including "The Talking Oak," "Ode to Memory," and "The
Lotos-Eaters." Cooke also produced a rimed tetrameter
version of "Tears, Idle Tears," but found his effort rather
unsatisfactory. The passing away of Poe affected him profoundly, and called forth several crude pieces lamenting the
lost genius. Most of these early efforts are somber. Virginia
is described as a land of lost ideals, of a fallen generation unworthy of being mentioned in the same breath with its ancestors. The youth wrote of "vain aspirings" and "vainer
labor," and discovered that "the soil of life" was "barren."

Like other dreamers in different ages, the young Virginian yearned for a panacea in some far off country with
a euphonic name. Just as Southey and his group looked
longingly to the banks of the Susquehanna, Cooke, living
near the ocean outlet of that river, looked in turn three
thousand miles to the West—to California. The idea of
going thither dominated his mind during the year 1849.
The Coleridgean plan of taking along a wife also received
rimed consideration. "Wattie" Leigh transferred a similar enthusiasm into action, for he went to California, where
he died a few years later. Any excessive ardor on Cooke's
part must, however, have been well discouraged by his
father, who is recorded as having said, apropos of the "vast
desert" and the "mountains above the clouds" which "sep-
erated" [sic] the East from the far West: "A strange
madness seems to have seized the country. This railroad to

the Pacific will really be built. And for what? Why to drain our very vital blood, our men and money into another country which nature has unchangeably forbidden to be a part of the United States.''

Cooke's life-long chivalric courtesy toward ladies was already being mistaken for affection, as he complains, but he wrote a goodly number of love-poems. He produced these effusions literally by the stop-watch, often recording the number of minutes required for a certain composition; hence the requirements of rime largely dictated the phraseology, and he was a ready victim for such conventional phrases as "eyes like stars" and "golden hair." But the poems reflect only one side of his intellectual life. He was not always experiencing "a bitter joy" or a "blissful pain." In addition to the attention to law, referred to in connection with his education, he was writing critiques of drama and music, taking notes from William Wirt on effective oratory, and unconsciously gathering from observation the materials for *Ellie* and certain of the Richmond scenes in *Surry* and *Mohun*. As the year 1849 differed little from those immediately preceding, it differed less from 1850. Cooke's lack of mental industry worried him. "Throw your soul into the drudgery, then it is not toil," he advised himself in his journal. The deaths of Philip in January, 1850, and of his mother later in the year may have completely unsettled him for a time. Such an effect was surely produced later by other deaths in his family. Leigh remonstrated with him about his gloominess. The year's chief literary advance came from a visit to the Berkeley Springs, where he took delight in certain old hunters whom he described as pure English with the soul of John Smith. The contrast between these men with their guns and the inn guests with their canes suggested a comparison of manners combined several years later with much else to make *Leather*

Stocking and Silk, which was his first publication in book form.

The 1849 diary and commonplace book indicated Cooke's strong yearning toward the profession of letters. He was amply justified, however, in his constant misgivings about following his literary bent, for he knew that he would have to be responsible for his entire support as soon as possible, and he must have known how pitifully hard it was for a Southern writer to earn a livelihood. Cooke became later perhaps the best paid Southern man of letters before 1870, yet, however much the youth may have believed in his talent, the future must have seemed dark. But it was easy to begin writing. There were few writers in the South then in comparison with the number in the North, the number in the South who with pen and ink sought food or justification after Appomattox, and the number everywhere now. And writers were really needed. Virginia was studded with newspapers many of which ran magazine features, and all of which required numerous special correspondents in default of the service of the modern news agencies. The writers of these communications occasionally received slight compensation, but usually none. The constantly precarious condition of Southern periodicals was due chiefly to poorly paying subscribers. It is indeed remarkable that so many gentlemen of the old régime should have considered it unimportant to pay for a book or magazine they had subscribed for. Perhaps books and magazines were regarded as, in the last analysis, mere ''scraps of paper.'' In any case the delinquency of supposed patrons constantly imperiled and assisted in snuffing out the periodical ventures of Southern editors. Even John Rogers Cooke, an honest, sober, lovable gentleman, was years behind in his subscription to the *Southern Literary Messenger* when his son's contributions served as payment. Know-

ing the difficulties which would beset his path, John Esten
Cooke, for eight years after his sixteenth year, withheld
a full devotion to the profession of letters. He attempted
in this indecision between law and literature the difficult
dual rôle which had proved so disastrous to the success and
happiness of his brother Philip.

In this hesitation between two careers, one galling but
probably profitable, the other agreeable but of little financial promise, Cooke's better energies went into his literary
efforts. At the age of eighteen he achieved the dignity of
print. "Avalon," a poem which appeared in the *Messenger*
for November, 1848, seems to have been his first published
article, and was followed in the next five years by a number
of unsigned or pseudonymous pieces. This early work was
not paid for, and Cooke justly never regarded it as professional; it merely afforded him the training available
to-day through college magazines. The ease with which he
secured a publisher, while it was an impetus to further composition, was detrimental to his artistic development. Many
of his less worthy efforts were accepted quite as readily as
his best, and he was soon ominously on the road to an
amazing productivity accompanied by an unfortunate dis-
taste for revision.

Cooke's early articles were of many types, and some of
them showed promise. In January, 1849, appeared the
prettily phrased, metrically correct "Eighteen Sonnets."
Each sonnet has a humorous twist, and is followed by a
prose paragraph pointing out its merit in a manner that
suggests a burlesque on some of the copiously edited modern
editions of poems. Cooke left no record of any share he may
have had in writing the short book notices which appeared
in the *Messenger*. That he was a conscientious, capable
critic, however, is shown by his "Thomas Carlyle and his
'Latter-Day Pamphlets,'" which appeared in the *Mes-*

senger in June, 1850. In clear, fluent language he sums
up the points made by Carlyle whom he considers to have
"crowned the column of political extravagance. . . .
Thomas Carlyle is now the head reformer of the age with
a perfectly distinct political theory of his own, and is soon,
we predict, to found a school of politics in England which
shall re-echo his wild doctrines. It ought to be called Car-
lyleism, for no other word will express it [*sic*] principles
so well. . . . In these papers, as throughout his entire
works, Carlyle, the man, stands prominent—a bold, earnest,
inflexible, conscientious thinker! . . . Whatever Carlyle advances, the world may take as his earnest true belief.''
The sonnet ''To Kossuth'' reflects the author's interest in
international affairs as well as affords a sample of his poetic
skill at this period:

TO KOSSUTH

O Kossuth, noble Kossuth! could the tears
　Of nations shed for thee enlarge thy fame
From Schumla's prison, which, through coming years,
　Shall stand the monument of Hapsburg's shame,
　Thine eagle eye, before to-morrow's sun,
　Would once more turn to thy dear Hungary
Far in the West, where shuddering upon
　Her mountain's rugged rim the sunsets die.
That eye of fire! Oh may it once again
　Inspire the mailéd breasts of serried hosts,
And flush ten thousand brows with proud disdain
　Of Austrian tyranny's vainglorious boasts.
May once more wave thy fiery plume on high—
　A morning star to night-steeped Hungary!

While balancing law and literature and producing short
articles, Cooke had found time to write two romances, *The
Knight of Espalion* and *Evan of Foix*. *The Knight of
Espalion* was written in the summer of 1847. ''My first
story and I think it pretty good,'' Cooke said of it years

later. This story, which has attracted attention because of the extreme youth of its author, was never published in book form, and did not find its way into the *Messenger* until 1860 when it was run as a serial from July to October. Much of Cooke's best work had appeared by 1860, so he wisely published the resurrected manuscript anonymously; it could have added nothing to his reputation. The story is without plot; it merely recounts certain adventures which befall Raoul d'Espalion, a companion in arms to the Viscount of Béziers. At the very beginning there is introduced in detail a troubadour to whom no further reference is made. An entire chapter is devoted to the love of Raoul for his cousin, but the topic is not again mentioned. On the whole, *The Knight of Espalion* gives the impression of being the first third of an unfinished story. Cooke was fascinated by the sonorous names of the Midi, and led his hero through nearly every town of importance. Except for a description of the wonderful Gothic portal of the Church of St. Gilles there is, however, not a trace of local color, and when Cooke glories in the autumn weather he obviously has in mind Virginia and not Southern France. The proof sheets of this story must never have come under the author's eye, for mistakes abound; to mention just a few, the river Aude is sometimes called the Ande, while the Ariège appears as the Aniege.

Evan of Foix, which was suggested by the *Froissart Ballads* of Philip and in particular by Cooke's reading of Dumas's *Agénor de Mauléon*, was begun in the fall of 1847 and finished the following spring. It was never published as a unit, but was "cut" into two parts, each of which appeared serially, unsigned, in the *Messenger*. *The Last Days of Gaston Phœbus, A Chronicle Not Found in Messire Jehan Froissart* ran from October, 1854, to January, 1855, and *A Kingdom Mortgaged* appeared monthly from May to September in the latter year. In scene, manner, and characters the *Evan of Foix* stories differ little from *The Knight of Espalion*. Their publication seems to have aroused no stir. In fact, mechanically, they may actually have caused their readers some annoyance; for *Gaston Phœbus* is ended with the cryptic note, "The sequel to the events just narrated, is properly reserved for another occasion," while the "to be continued" or "to be concluded" was thrice left off the installments of *A Kingdom Mortgaged*. These stories have slight kinship if any with the author's novels of the following decade. For his next fiction of book length Cooke turned from a distant century and a far-off unknown land to the very Virginia border which as a child he knew from observation and tradition.

Cooke may have given some attention to the private study of law in 1850, for his long and uncongenial apprenticeship was soon to be merged into constantly irksome and unsuccessful practice. "On the 27th of February [1851]," he recorded in his diary, "I hung out my sign—or rather mine and Pa's, for it runs 'John R. Cooke & Jno. Esten Cooke: Law Office'—at a cost of two dollars, and yesterday Brown offered me two cases." A later entry says: "I commenced the practice of law on the first day of March." Perhaps Cooke qualified that day, since his entry for March 2 refers to his fulfilling this requirement without embarrassment though he was, as he puts it, the "observed of all observers." His first case came in April and he spoke for three quarters of an hour, receiving the approval of friends present, but not pleasing himself. The dread of losing his poise must have obsessed him, for he again with satisfaction recalls his calmness. Law became even more irksome to the lawyer than it had been to the student. Because of his desultory, unguided study Cooke now felt imperatively the need of continual application. He resolved on this again and again, but always failed. For twelve months after his admittance to the bar, he vowed to quit writing, but could not. Writing and smoking went hand in hand and he condemned them together. Such passages as the following abound in his journal: "I do not study (law). My mind is thoroughly dissipated, and I only dream and scheme like an oriental without *doing* anything. Tobacco is partly the cause and that knocks in the head all calm, quiet application as completely as opium. I am alternately raised to the heavens and sunk into a horrible depression of spirits. I am ridiculous in my thoughts, irrational in my calculations, start at the least sudden noise, and magnify every molehill into a mountain, into an Alps. My whole life is alternately a train of dreamy, delightful reveries, under the effect of coffee and tobacco after breakfast, and, when that effect is worn off, of depressed foreboding misery. Now I swear to change all this. I cannot at once give up tobacco, more especially when going to the country where there is so much idleness. But on my return, with the assistance of God, I will throw this present life to the dogs. I will be fixed in my room and I will study law, history and the modern languages. I will discipline my mind and throw 'general literature' to the devil. I will smoke moderately and never write. . . . But also I will never scheme out literary undertakings. Tobacco makes me irritable. . . . I will never more be so completely under its influence. With the first day of January 1852 I commence a new life *ab initio*. May God give me strength to keep my resolution."

Many circumstances combined to render impossible a strict adherence to this proposed regimen. In the first place Cooke allowed himself such loopholes as "in moderation," and invariably decided to begin his severe self-discipline not directly but at some future date—in this case after twenty-eight days. In his abnegations he always allowed himself society as a necessity, and society at this period of his life led to serenades, suppers with young men at the hotels, soda water with girl cousins, and the opera. These diversions afforded material for description, but did not further a knowledge of law. Such of his friends as remembered the old Franklin Debating Society days advised him to be an out-and-out man of letters. The little daughters of Philip, to whom he wrote often on pretty note paper and sent many presents, wanted most of all to read something else written by their ''dear, dear uncle.'' And if the prospects of a support by his pen were chimerical, he would at least have less aggressive competition in writing than in law, and he had made an approved start. He was already one of the mainstays of the *Messenger*, and edited the March, 1851, number for John Reuben Thompson.

Thompson and Cooke were intimate associates at this time; they visited the river islands, walked again and again across the Danville bridge, and were invited together to country homes. One of Thompson's most interesting poems is ''A Letter,'' addressed to his friend who was enjoying the country in August, 1852, while the editor sweltered in Richmond. The question of pay for Cooke's articles seems, nevertheless, to have been a delicate one. Cooke felt that if his productions were good enough for the *Messenger* to print by the dozen they ought to be worth something. ''If he expects me to write for him forever he's mistaken— without some remuneration. I like him, however, and shall avoid any quarrel, which I do not anticipate but am ready for.'' ''I want money most confoundedly and Thompson is or says he is so poor that all hope from that quarter is gone.''

As time went on, Cooke's vows to cease writing became more and more vehement but were the more easily broken. Finally he allowed himself to write when on visits, then short pieces in Richmond, and soon, even in Richmond, longer articles the composition of which produced no nervous excitement. He had, meanwhile, begun to seek recognition in the North. He had met and had been encouraged by Rufus W. Griswold, who contemplated an edition of the "Works" of Philip. Submitting a paper on Poe,[1] whom he had heard as a lecturer and knew as a gossiped-about figure of note in the city, he had tried for, anticipated, and failed to receive one of Sartain's prizes. A letter to the editor of *Godey's* brought the reply that the magazine had enough manuscripts on hand "for two years." The Harpers, however, accompanied a rejection with a courteous intimation of willingness to see other pieces. Cooke began a story at once. "This is not breaking my resolution," he concluded, "I always excepted writing for pay." A few weeks later the following entry was made in the journal: "On the 10th of March [1852] I received from Harper and Bros. $10 for 'Barry and Courtlandt the Tall,' the first money I ever got for fiction[2] writing." This was the price which Cooke had set upon the manuscript. He received it at a time when it assisted his sick father, a circumstance which he always considered of good omen. Thompson also was willing to pay when forced to the wall. The next entry in the diary records that he took "Peony" at $1.50 a page. Cooke became thus, almost in spite of himself, a professional man of letters.

[1] Edgar Allan Poe went to Richmond in 1849 "to deliver his lecture on 'The Poetic Principle' which I had the pleasure of hearing. The lecturer stood in a graceful attitude, leaning one hand on a small table beside him, and his wonderfully clear and musical voice speedily brought the audience under its spell." — J. E. C. in his journal.

[2] The use of the word "fiction" does not imply that Cooke had received pay for other forms of composition; he had, however, because of his excellent penmanship, earned money as a copyist.

CHAPTER II

GENTLEMAN AND NOVELIST OF OLD VIRGINIA

WHEN John Reuben Thompson bought the *Southern Literary Messenger* in the fall of 1847, he announced in the October number that he would continue the practice of law. In 1852 Cooke entertained a similar idea, but, like Thompson, dismissed it in a very short time. In these days of his dwindling neglected practice he received from David Strother a good-natured taunting letter of congratulation on a supposed fee of a thousand dollars. Apparently the last trace of Cooke's legal career came a few years later when Derby and Jackson, publishers of *The Last of the Foresters,* asked him to act as their attorney in a case involving the failure of a Richmond bookseller. The definite assumption of a literary career produced little change in Cooke's life. As he grew older and better known, he naturally figured more largely in the intellectual circles of Richmond; but, because of the salability of his writings and his varied duties, he nearly neglected his journal. In fact he expressly states that for three years in the late fifties he kept no record whatever of his thoughts and performances. Enough information is available, however, to prevent any interruption in the continuity of his life-story.

Cooke's sisters had already married when his mother died in 1850; so the father relinquished the house he had been occupying and became a roomer and boarder. "The Clifton" was for some time the joint home of the father and son, but much of the latter's work at this time was done in a quiet room set aside for his use by Mammy Giddy in her house in "Gullination," a low section of Richmond. John Esten later occupied quarters on Eleventh Street at "Goddin's," a rooming-house which subsequently housed the Confederate States Post Office. He also spent some time at the Richmond home of the Duvals, the family into which his sister Sal had married.

Cooke's work in the fifties was interrupted by no serious illness, but he was often troubled with a provoking neuralgia of the teeth, a worry from which he was destined never to be free. He complained also of a nervousness which he fortunately outgrew as time went on. His use of tobacco no longer prompted such violent resolutions, but letters from members of his family still counseled moderation, lest he inflict upon himself "some organic disease." In his early twenties Cooke wore for a time a full beard and "long cavalier hair." Describing this in his journal he complains terribly of heat, the most patent advantage of being a roundhead seeming never to have occurred to him. He subsequently reduced his beard to the mustache and imperial which he wore in later life.

Among Cooke's papers there is a memorandum giving a detailed expense account for the year 1852. From this it may be learned that he was a subscriber to the Richmond *Dispatch*, bought the first two monthly numbers of *Bleak House*, bought an occasional *Harper's*, which he would later send to friends in the Valley, and attended the theatre some twenty times. His greatest dissipation of the year was occasioned by a visit to Richmond of the well-known theatrical family, the Batemans. He saw them perform more than a half-dozen times, bought bonbons for the child-actresses, and finally purchased a picture of them in *The Young Couple*. The gifts to "Mammy" totaled $4.65 for nine months. Some of the items are humorous as well as autobiographical, for example: "mint juleps...25, cursed folly." Such entries, however, were not numerous, those for drink totaling much less than those for tobacco, while the latter amounted to only some six or seven dollars for the nine months spent in Richmond. Cooke perhaps drank more at Christmas time than usual as the following "memo" would suggest: "In drinking sweet drinks, 'bottom' with grog and 'top off' with the same. I did last night and am fresh as a lark: decidedly important *mem.* about Xmas." The year's expenses totaled four hundred and eighty-five dollars. "Is it possible?" Cooke asks. "But old board and new clothes make it: and so it is no fair exhibit of my expenditure. A new leaf this 1853!"

Cooke's Christmases and summers were usually spent with relatives or friends living near the Valley home of his childhood. He seems to have gone every October to visit in Amelia County the Stegers, the marriage family of his sister Mary. In these journeys and visits he was extending the knowledge of Virginia which he had begun to acquire in boyhood from stories told by his father and had later developed by eager and wide study. All his experiences afforded subjects for the numerous articles he was now producing. Historical narratives, as well as fictitious ones, were based on his well-loved *History of the Valley of Virginia* by Kercheval, supplemented by a first-hand knowledge of the lower Valley. The familiarity with Fairfax and Washington family history and legend served as a basis for "Early Haunts of Washington," in the *New York Times*, for the handsomely illustrated "Greenway Court" which was featured in *Putnam's* for June, 1857, and for a romance which ran as a serial in the *Messenger* and was later issued in book form as *Fairfax*. A journey from Richmond to the Valley by the water route resulted in a sonnet, "Sunset on the Chesapeake." "For my trip to

Amelia," he wrote in his soon to be neglected diary, "see 'A Handful of Autumn Leaves' in the December [1852] *Messenger.*" The article here referred to was a collection of seven short easy-chair essays: "In the Woods," "Some Authors and Books," "Embers of a Wood Fire," "Old and New Songs," "Sunlight, Winds and Music," "The Enthusiastic Sportsman," "The End of Autumn"—titles which illustrate the turn Cooke's talent was taking at this period. He was fond of historical fact, but he liked to contemplate it in terms of romance. He was not only a literary critic but a critic of manners who saw in the past fine ideals which had been sadly departed from. This theme afforded him the material for several magazine articles; his first contribution to *Putnam's* (August, 1853) actually bore the title, "Virginia Past and Present." Exceedingly modern seems "Minuet and Polka" with its reference to the "arm around the waist, the breath upon the cheek, the head upon the shoulder." The author, of course, presents a brief for the old-fashioned dance: "The minuet was delicacy, courtesy, lofty-toned respect—in one word— chivalry." Cooke was a skilful literary parodist. He was the author of the "Unpublished Mss. from the Portfolios of the Most Celebrated Authors. By Motley Ware, Esq.," which the Duyckinck brothers published in the *Literary World* during 1853. Along with the burlesques of Carlyle, Dumas, and others Cooke solemnly included one of himself, or rather of such of his work as had appeared under his pseudonym, "Pen Ingleton, Esq." With unerring instinct he chose as a likely subject his great fondness for autumn: "The flutter and glitter of the golden autumn leaves are once more in my eyes and in my heart."

In addition to his abundant and varied work for periodicals, Cooke began toward the close of 1852 his first serious effort as a novelist. *Leather Stocking and Silk; or, Hunter*

John Myers and his Times. A Story of the Valley of Virginia [1] was finished the following spring and its author, having gone in May as far as New York with "Wattie" Leigh on the latter's way to California, arranged with the Harpers for its publication. Cooke experienced keen joy in correcting the proof, which he received in Virginia in driblets; but when the book was on the eve of its appearance the Harper fire destroyed everything except a stereotyped impression preserved in a vault. The author first learned of the fire from the *New York Times*—which of course did not print a list of the contents of the vault—and despairingly believed that his labor had been in vain. The Harper presses were soon going again, however, and the summer of 1854 saw the appearance of *Leather Stocking and Silk.*

Irving was the literary grand old man of Cooke's youth, and *Leather Stocking and Silk* owes him more than a little. Contemporary American critics seem not to have noticed this debt to the author of the *Sketch-Book*, but the London *Athenæum* referred to it and Cooke admitted it. The names of several important characters are Dutch. The style of the book is Irvingesque, particularly in passages which contrast the old with the new in the life of the Virginia border. Many of the chapters are little more than genial "familiar" essays wholly unnecessary for the advance of the plot. The Cooper influence was more obvious but less subtle. The "Leatherstocking Tales" suggested the title, and as a border tale the novel belongs to the school in which Cooper holds primacy.

This initial volume exemplifies Professor Brander Matthews's statement that an author, in his first book, tries to tell everything he knows. Cooke himself says of the genesis of *Leather Stocking and Silk*: "The story was suggested

[1] In this and other titles, Cooke's punctuation has been retained.

by my father's account of old Hunter John Myers, whom he had known—and I worked into it the scenes of Barry; old traditions I had heard of some people playing cards on a tombstone of the old Martinsburg Church, seizing and fleeing on a fine mare of my grandfather Pendleton, etc. In drawing Max, Jr., I had my dear Buck Lyons in mind, and M. Pantoufle was Pa's fencing master, M. Xaupi.'' The student of Cooke's life can see clearly the sources of many other elements of the book. It shows a kinship with his magazine essays and stories. In the case of the ''Scenes of Barry'' the adaptation was so complete that Cooke ''bought back'' from the Harpers the article for which he had first received pay. The Bateman children inspired the theatrical scene in which little Sally plays a star part. The long speech of the old negro woman is a tribute to Cooke's negro ''mammy.'' The career of the elder Max, who goes away from the Valley and returns to it a distinguished man, parallels in part that of his creator. A fondness for Richter, expressed in the autobiography, is seen in the chapter named for that writer. Some of Cooke's own poems are interpolated as the compositions of one of the characters.

Leather Stocking and Silk is, in spite of its scant four hundred pages, divided into three parts and ninety-five chapters. As might be expected from such a structure and the heterogeneity of sources, the plot—here sketched in briefest outline—is somewhat weak. Maximilian Courtlandt is in love with his cousin, Nina Von Horn, who, however, marries a solemn, self-important but promising lawyer named Lyttleton. Max has a small brother, Barry, who loves Sally, the little daughter of Hunter John. Five years elapse. Max returns from Paris a doctor of medicine and goes everywhere in the neighborhood, but no one knows him until he chooses to reveal his identity. Barry marries

Sally Myers, and Max marries Nina, now a consolable
widow of two years' standing. Twenty years pass. Nina
has died and Max marries Miss Josephine Emberton, whom
he knew in his youth. Barry now has two daughters, one
of whom marries a brother of Miss Emberton, the other
marrying Max, Jr., Max's only son. Hunter John, who
remembers the Indians, and M. Pantoufle, the dancing-
master, come through the three parts without matrimonial
entanglements and die at the end. Such a frame-work
could hardly be the basis of a great composition, but *Leather
Stocking and Silk* possessed some real merits which pointed
to better subsequent work. The easy, graceful, flowing
style is little inferior to the author's best achievement. The
book has a certain value as social history. Some of the
conversations sparkle; they are essentially transcripts from
life, as may be seen from actual conversations recorded in
the diaries. Cooke prided himself upon the accuracy of his
delineation of Hunter John, who saw the pines cut down
to make the main street of Martinsburg, and yet lived to
see a polite society, with its appurtenances and conventions,
press forward upon the receding frontier. Even then on
the border were met the characters Cooke loved best to
draw: "elegantly dressed ladies, radiant with rich falling
lace, and supporting on their white foreheads curiously
fashioned towers of hair; gracefully attentive gentlemen
with powdered locks, stiff-collared coats, and silk stockings
and knee-buckles." Not even Barry—ill-tempered young
bully that he is—can dissipate the atmosphere of kindliness
which pervades the entire composition, and reflects the tem-
perament of the genial author, who says "to the reader:"
"If the book be found entertaining and (above all else)
the spirit of it pure, the writer will be more than satisfied."
The first of these wishes was perhaps not realized. *Leather
Stocking and Silk* split in halves the great decade which

began with *Vanity Fair* and ended with *Adam Bede;* but Cooke, unlike his fellow-countryman Hawthorne, did not share largely in the great novel-writing power then abroad in the English-speaking world. Fitting it is, however, that the second wish should have been expressed in the preface of his first book. It was fulfilled to the letter. In a score of novels and hundreds of shorter compositions he did not make use of an impure word or situation.

When *Leather Stocking and Silk* was accepted by the Harpers, its author at once began another frontier romance which dealt with figures of such historical importance as the sixth Lord Fairfax and the youthful George Washington. The historical period of the new work antedated that of the first novel by about fifty years, and for his background Cooke relied abundantly upon Kercheval. *Fairfax,* as the book was eventually called, bears as a border romance a kinship to *Leather Stocking and Silk,* and as a colonial romance points to the author's third book, *The Virginia Comedians.* The germ of the latter so fascinated Cooke that he dropped the nearly finished *Fairfax* in the fall of 1853 and devoted himself to the more newly conceived work. The abandoned novel was completed in May, 1858, and was published in the *Messenger* from April to December the following year as *Greenway Court; or, The Bloody Ground.* With very slight changes the serial was issued in volume form by Carleton in 1868 under the title of *Fairfax: or, The Master of Greenway Court. A Chronicle of the Valley of the Shenandoah.*

Cooke left no record of exactly how much of Fairfax was yet to be done when he first laid it aside, but it is probable that the very dramatic conclusion was written later. The work is markedly more entertaining than *Leather Stocking and Silk* and is a not wholly unworthy forerunner of *The Virginia Comedians.* A youthful love-affair of Washington, who found time to survey the maidens as well as the earl's domain; the ensnaring by a "Lamia" of Falconbridge and Fairfax, who turn out to be son and father; the prowess and the courting of a robust "Injun"-hating Captain Wagner: these are the ingredients of the plot. The dénouement is precipitated by an Indian raid and a reprisal imitated closely from *The Last of the Mohicans.* Here, as in Cooper's tale, death solves the problem of the noble red youth who loves beyond the bounds of his race. There is, too, an exceedingly fascinating woman, a combination on a more refined plane of Judith and Hetty Hutter; though, unfortunately, Bertha Argal's insanity is narrated rather than actually depicted. To the unsuspecting reader, she is merely rather witchingly endowed with "those wiles which it is the sad misfortune of woman to possess," as she herself states after the author finally declares her criminally insane. An epilogue handles effectively a scene in which the aged Fairfax learns shortly before his death that his former protégé, "that curly-pate," has destroyed British dominion in Virginia. A great weakness of Cooke's historical fiction is in *Fairfax* seen for the first time. In treating actual persons he does not always distinguish between what might have happened and what is generally known not to have happened. He discredits the essential historical truth of his narrative by giving a son to the bachelor Fairfax.

The annual state fair held in Richmond about the first of November has long been a rather notable occasion for the people of the city and the state. In 1853 the event was of much more than usual significance for John Esten Cooke. A full-fledged author now, patronized by the Harpers, he attended the fair with Thompson and Paul Hayne, the latter being on a visit from Charleston. But the crowning event was the presence of the Batemans, whose previous visits Cooke remembered most pleasantly, since he had known intimately the little actresses who had afforded "the very atmosphere in which the adventures of Max were shaped." Bateman was, as usual, most cordial to Cooke and invited him to dine. "Kate and Ellen remembered me spite of the ten thousand faces they have since seen . . . children will not stay children: the little girls are taller, their faces less round and infantile, their acting less the vagary of children. Well, so be it: but one great and happy change I observed in Kate. At those unworthy double-entendres in the *Young Couple* she did not smile . . . and seemed to be ashamed . . . went through the part with manifest repugnance. Poor child! She is getting old enough to feel as an incipient woman the unworthy part she plays. Thank heaven for it and may they both soon leave the stage and become children again." Cooke went to see them often. He carried them "little cologne kegs," candy, and books. "I am in love with Kate, the charming little rascal with the bright eyes and curls, and sharp talk, too!" Cooke even spoke to the father about the advisability of the girls' discontinuing their stage careers. Bateman assured him of an intention to settle within a year on a place he owned near Cincinnati, but his declared intention was distrusted by Cooke,—justly, as events proved.

The idea of making literary use of Kate Bateman and her profession was first suggested by a paragraph which Cooke clipped from the odds-and-ends column of a newspaper, and later pasted in his scrapbook: "The first play performed in America by a regular company of commedians [*sic*] was the 'Merchant of Venice,' at Williamsburg, the capital of Virginia, on the 5th of September, 1762 [*sic*]. The commedians under the management of Mr. Hallam[1] em-

---

[1] The Hallam here referred to was Lewis, a brother of the English theatrical manager, William Hallam. Lewis Hallam's company be-

barked in the Charming Sally, Capt. Lee, early in the month of May of that year, and after a voyage of six weeks, a short passage in those days, arrived safely in Yorktown, Virginia.'' Some of these statements are not true, of course, but the clipping served to connect Cooke's dominant interest in Kate Bateman with the Colonial period which he had long worshiped and was already ambitiously preparing to treat historically. His visualization of Kate Bateman as a heroine took the author back into the past with a dashing enthusiasm which made *The Virginia Comedians* by far the finest of his books.

A few days after seeing the seminal paragraph, Cooke ''constructed the whole story'' of *The Virginia Comedians*. ''It only remains to do the mechanical part,'' he wrote in his journal. He was advancing slowly, when on December 23 a letter from the Harpers announced that the plates of *Leather Stocking and Silk* had been saved. ''Hurrah!'' he wrote, ''I trusted in Providence and am repaid.'' He threw away his three-page false start and, beginning anew with a vigor which never abated, finished the first book at eleven o'clock at night on February 8, 1854, and the entire work by March 3. He found great joy in his labor. ''The *Virginia Comedians* has stopped this journal—never have I worked so hard. I have done 100 pages a day repeatedly.''[1] He also realized that he was producing a notable composition. ''Mr. Effingham and Beatrice are what I wanted them to be, and I have developed their characters to my satisfaction. The incidents are full of dramatic effect—Charles's

gan its American career with "The Merchant of Venice" at Williamsburg, September 5, 1752. For interesting details, see *William Dunlap*, by Oral Sumner Coad. (New York, The Dunlap Society, 1917.)

[1] Throughout his life Cooke preferred to write upon sheets of paper about five by eight inches.

colloquies with Henry among my best writing. Lanky and Mr. Crow are developed to my satisfaction and the penultimate chapter is to my taste—I doubted about it as I did about killing Beatrice. But the book had to end with an idea: and death crowns her. . . . The book will hit I think if ever published. . . . It is my best work.''

Cooke's pride was justified and his intense application was rewarded. *The Virginia Comedians: or, Old Days in the Old Dominion* was published in two volumes by D. Appleton and Company in 1854, and was several times reprinted. Since 1916 it has been out of print, but it deserves to be kept alive. It should be neglected by no serious student of American fiction. It is of value to the social historian, is interesting to the student of the early American theater, and should prove fascinating to those who take delight in things pre-Revolutionary. At the opening of the thirty-second chapter of the second book Cooke states that he "aims at presenting in a brief and rapid manner, some view, however slight, of the various classes of individuals who formed that Virginia of 1765.'' This inclusion of "various classes'' marked a decided advance in Virginia fiction, the writers of which had seen in Colonial Virginia chiefly cavaliers and servants. The low-class characters are not, however, successfully drawn. They either are meagerly sketched, lack the appearance of reality, or are portrayed merely in a subordinate relation to some superior person. Cooke was never skilful in his delineation of the negro. With the exception of Mr. Crow, an uncommon type, negroes serve in *The Virginia Comedians* almost solely as bridle-rein receivers for dismounting "cavaliers.''

With these reservations Cooke achieved his aims notably. The middle-class Waters family is well portrayed. The upper part of society is brilliantly depicted. The bluff old head of Effingham Hall, known everywhere as a prime aris-

tocrat, slouches and hobnobs as he pleases with no loss of
dignity, but expects all views to take color from his: "Every
man a vote! Who speaks of it? Who broaches such an
absurdity?" His interlocutor hastens to say "a parcel of
hair-brained [sic] young men," and diverts the storm from
his own head, though not preventing it entirely. The Hall
also shelters the prim and precise Miss Alethea, who, though
a severe censor of others, is none the less staging a sub-rosa
romance of her own, as she hastens to explain when she is
discovered in the act of kissing. The Squire's younger
son, a budding duplicate of his father, industriously courts
his twelve-year-old first cousin, an orphan now adopted into
the family.

The eldest son is the hero or villain of the first volume of
the book. Champ Effingham is just back from the "grand
tour" on which he has indulged violently in "every species
of dissipation." He is mortally bored by Virginia and
everything in it, and shows his contempt upon every occasion. He dashes books around, kicks dogs, and deports himself generally as might be expected of the lowest type of
eighteenth century buck. It is obvious, though, that he is
going to tame down and marry Clare Lee, his childhood
sweetheart. He is a little slow, however, in arranging matters, partly because of his father's loud insistence upon the
marriage and partly because of the obvious willingness of
the colorless Clare. Progress in the affair is at last being
made; but soon a theatrical troupe comes to Williamsburg.
During a performance of a play, Effingham leaves the side
of the mortified Clare, mounts the stage and accosts Beatrice
Hallam, the beautiful star of the company. Rebuffed, he
is the laughing-stock of the audience. Borne on by a carefully self-encouraged whirlwind of rage and passion, he
determines to overcome the young girl, and easily becomes
intimate with Hallam, her supposed father, who compels her

to receive him. After torturing her with his importunings, even insultingly offering to marry her, he finds that force is the only resort, and carries her off at night across his saddle to the James River, where two hireling thugs have placed a boat at his disposal. Previously, however, Beatrice has been for a sail on the James, has had her boat capsized, and has been rescused by young Charles Waters. The latter—whom she has found to be her cousin, the son of the brother of her real father—learns of the abduction, and with one helper pursues Effingham. When the boats meet, the rescuers put one of their adversaries out of commission, but Effingham attempts to murder Waters, who is sustaining the fainting girl. The reeling of the vessel, however, causes him to miss his mark and strike down his surviving man. He then plunges his sword into the breast of Waters, shoots Beatrice, jumps into the river and swims for the shore. He hastens out of the country, for he doubtless realizes that for so dastardly an action even Mr. Effingham can not go unpunished. After long suffering Waters recovers and marries Beatrice, who has not been quite so badly hurt as he, but whose night's experience, added to a previous cough, is enough to forebode her subsequent death from consumption.

The second book brings Effiingham back to Virginia. He has again been wallowing in the sties of European cities, and comes home a grumbling, vitality-sapped household tyrant. His friends (he actually has them) are still determined to inflict him upon poor, stupid Clare Lee, and this time their generalship is successful. They cause him to suspect that she is being courted by another, and at the proper time the little ever-willing ewe-lamb is fed to the Minotaur. So much for Clare and Champ Effingham, and Beatrice and Charles Waters, who are the central characters of the first volume.

The Virginia Comedians would, however, scarcely be a mid-nineteenth-century novel if it stopped at so small an amount of love complication. Miss Alethea and the jolly fox-hunting Jack Hamilton, Lanky Lugg and Donsy Smith, Captain Ralph Waters and Henrietta Lee all tread the path of matrimony. When the two parts of *The Virginia Comedians* were issued by the G. W. Dillingham Company as separate novels they were called *Beatrice Hallam* and *Captain Ralph,* respectively. In fact, with Beatrice ill in the mountains and with the Champ-Clare affair so lukewarm, the courtship of Captain Ralph and Henrietta is the real life of the second book. Lanky is Ralph's servant, and the wedding of the musical, good-natured, honest but not very capable youth to the sweet daughter of the Williamsburg factor is largely owing to the good offices of the indefatigable captain.

Nearly all of Cooke's novels belong to the type in which heredity and surroundings, if used at all, are mere conventions to be juggled with at the caprice of the author. There is in *The Virginia Comedians* a contrast between the serious, contemplative, revolution-fomenting Charles Waters and his brother, the boisterous soldier-adventurer, Ralph. The lily-pale Clare is a sister of Henrietta, who is as robust, aggressive, and sprightly as need be. Ralph is quite below Henrietta in social rank, but he stands on his merit, and is welcomed by both father and daughter, though not quite so promptly by the latter. The courtship of these lively, sensible people gives a sane tone to the second book which, however, is not so dramatic as the first. Apart from the main plot *The Virginia Comedians* offers some interesting digressions in the way of comic scenes and sketches from colonial life. Tag as parson and schoolmaster is well conceived. Notable also are the accounts of the governor's ball,

the Williamsburg fair, and the development of liberal sentiment in politics.

If a prospective reader decides from the first few pages
whether or not he will go on with a book, John Esten Cooke
is under a disadvantage. *The Virginia Comedians* is supposed to be arranged from or based on a manuscript work
written by a Mr. C. Effingham, who refers to Champ as
his "respected ancestor," but is otherwise not identified.
Cooke as editor begins with a few pages supposedly by the
"author of the ms.," and then explains that he will sim-
plify, "give more artistic point to certain passages," and
omit some "unnecessary and superfluous portions." This
complex beginning, which may have been suggested to
Cooke by Carlyle's *Sartor Resartus,* is likely to perplex
the casual reader and is unfortunately characteristic of
many of the author's books. But Cooke here plays up to
the part admirably. Few writers who shift from one supposed character to another are more skilful in escaping
a stylistic identity. The pretended "author" begins one
passage: " 'Have you never, O friend, who now readest these
unworthy lines, abandoned for a time your city life, with
its noise and bustle, and eternal striving, and locking up
with your ledgers, or your lawbooks, all thoughts of business, gone into that bright lowland which the James flows
proudly through, a band of silver wavering across a field
of emerald? . . .' " At the close of this passage the supposed "editor" says: "Thus far, the author of the ms. in
that rhetorical and enthusiastic style which everywhere
characterizes his works. Let us descend from the heights
of apostrophe and declamation to the prose of simple narrative." And he does so.

Aside from being Cooke's best work, *The Virginia Comedians* is his longest—and the later *Henry St. John* makes
virtually the third volume of a trilogy. In these novels

Cooke preserves a superb detachment; he rarely if at all intrudes his personality. It is hard even to think of Champ Effingham without bitterness, but Cooke had studied his field and, without apology or praise, presented his characters as he conceived them to have existed. In this respect his work is on a plane with *Tom Jones* and *Vanity Fair*, and such an achievement is an artistic triumph for a writer who found *The Wide, Wide World* "one of the most delightful of books," and was soon to write a novel of this once popular type.

From its very appearance in the year of its completion *The Virginia Comedians* was favorably received, flattering reviews appearing in the Charleston, Richmond, and New York papers, and in *Harper's Magazine*. In "Virginia," a Phi Beta Kappa poem, delivered at William and Mary College on July 3, 1856, Thompson paid a graceful tribute to its vivid recreation of the colonial past. The fame of the novel was such that it was dramatized by C. W. Tayleure and presented at the Richmond Theatre, Richmond, on April 29, 1857. Joseph Jefferson, almost on the threshold of his great fame, was stage manager and played the part of Lanky Lugg, the rôle best suited to his talents. "In consequence of the extreme length of this great play no other piece can be presented." So reads the program from which it is learned that Patrick Henry—who in the book is unrevealed by name until the end—was made into the star part and was played by Mr. W. H. Briggs. The play was shortly thereafter presented at the Holliday Street Theatre, Baltimore, the book title having been discarded in favor of "Freedom's Dawn, or the Man in the Red Cloak." In a Baltimore announcement Tayleure referred to the play's "marked favor of reception" in Richmond; but it seems never to have been revived. It was Cooke's only work to appear on the professional stage. His novels have far too many characters, too much sweep and pageantry, for successful condensation in a three-hour talking piece. If the cinema had existed in his time he might have won fame and fortune as a scenario writer. His crises are normally brought about by accidents, runaways, or rescues from drowning, rather than by the subtleties of conversation or the development of a mental attitude. In their shift back and forth from public events to the fortunes of a set of lovers, Cooke's best books before and after the war are of the same mold as the motion picture, *The Birth of a Nation*.

During his hard work on *The Virginia Comedians* Cooke had thought frequently of joining the church. He was by nature of a religious turn of mind; and, on the death of his mother and several times thereafter, had received letters from relatives urging him to take the step. Cooke's father was not a member of the church; his mother had been an Episcopalian, and to her church he turned. The event is beautifully commemorated in his diary: "Last Sunday—March 5—I joined St. James's Church. It is the greatest event of my life and I devoutly thank God for having changed my heart and made me see the sublime light of heaven. Henceforth, I feel, the world has no trial too hard for endurance—death no sting. . . . A feeling of perfect peace follows and accompanies me—life spreading before me like a boundless horizon of sunshine. . . . Singular! I was just finishing the *Va. Comedians* and on Saturday morning rose with my head full of the revision. Then commenced the struggle whether I should go on with it or write at once to Mr. Cummins to ask an interview. The hand of God is just as plain to me in the whole matter as that sunshine yonder. I wrote: that I wished to see him—thought of joining the church, doubted my fitness. He would be most pleased to see me. I went: had an hour's talk—he had never seen a state of feeling which delighted

him more . . . tomorrow was communion! There it was:
had I delayed to this week I should not now have been
a member of the church. . . . All my friends are surprised
and delighted—Buck I think much impressed. Would to
God Pa, and he and all would be made to think by it. My
life has only begun—the world opened. My heart and intellect take a new glory, and I shall be a celebrated man.
. . . One thing comes to my mind often. . . . My blessed,
sainted mother who placed her hand on my head as she was
dying and blessed me—whose last prayer I doubt not was
for her children—Mother, I have taken one step toward
you.'' Letters, journals, and his books testify to the never-
waning quality of Cooke's Christian faith. The step here
recorded colored the rest of his life.

Thomas Jefferson had written the statute of Virginia for
religious freedom which struck a staggering blow at. the
Episcopal church; but this fact did not prevent Cooke from
finding in the early life of the great statesman the inspiration for his next literary venture. Almost immediately
upon finishing *The Virginia Comedians* Cooke began, using
the same locality and the same period of time, to fashion a
slender romance around certain letters and other accounts
of Thomas Jefferson's sojourn at William and Mary College. He said of *The Youth of Jefferson* that it was ''written as a relaxation'' from ''the exhausting toil'' which attended the composition of the preceding work; and it is
neither very wide in scope nor very ambitious. *The Virginia Comedians* and *Henry St. John* together constitute
an epic of late Colonial Virginia. With reference to these
works the brief *Youth of Jefferson* is, as it were, an expanded interlude, a relation borne later by *Hilt to Hilt* to
Surry of Eagle's-Nest and its sequel, *Mohun*. As in the
case of so many of Cooke's books, the title was hard to
choose. *Crooks and Shepherds* yielded place to *Arcadians,*

under which name the manuscript was sent to Redfield on
May 19. It appeared, however, as *The Youth of Jefferson;
or a Chronicle of College Scrapes at Williamsburg, in Virginia, A.D., 1764.* On a visit to New York, Cooke engaged
a bookseller in conversation with regard to the book which
was displayed for sale. The incognito author was much
amused at the almost angry insistence that the work was
an authoritative history. Aside from the three books published and the three he wrote, the year 1854 found Cooke
active in other ways. "I am for the first time very busy
regularly," he wrote. "For a week or so I have been attending to *Middleton's Case,* and editing the *Messenger* and
ditto the *Express,* and writing the *Arcadians.* Very tiresome, but it will advantage me."

The Youth of Jefferson affords pleasant reading for
those who like a quaintly imagined reconstruction of the
past and are not averse to having historical personages doc-
tored to suit a novelist's purposes. The future author of
the Declaration of Independence was in love with Rebecca
Burwell. Miss Burwell, however, married Jacqueline Ambler, and Jefferson later married Martha Wayles, the widow
of Bathurst Skelton. So much for the actual historical basis
of the romance. In Cooke's handling of the Jefferson-
Ambler-Burwell triangle, the embryo sage of Monticello
appears as Sir Asinus, his rival as Jacques, and the lady
as Belle-bouche or Belinda, a name which Jefferson actually employed in referring to Miss Burwell. Cooke makes
use of non-historical characters as well as historical. He
describes the governor's surroundings at Williamsburg, the
life of the college, and the plantation life of the neighborhood. Of course these accounts are not definitely authentic,
although an atmosphere of essential truth pervades the
work. "If its grotesque incidents beguile an otherwise
weary hour with innocent laughter, the writer's ambition

will have been fully gratified,'' says the author in his six-line preface. Cooke's humor is never of the broad, racy kind which is often regarded as typical of the United States; it is delicate, playful, fanciful, at most provocative of a smile. A short quotation will illustrate the tone of the composition:

"'Please hand me the music,' said Belle-bouche; 'there in the scarlet binding.'

"Jacques started and obeyed. As she received it the young girl's hand touched his own and he uttered a sigh which might have melted rocks. The reason was, that Jacques was in love; we state the fact, though it has probably appeared before.

"Belle-bouche's voice was like liquid moonlight and melodious flowers. Its melting involutions and expiring cadences unwound themselves and floated from her lips like satin ribbon gradually drawn out."

Cooke followed fast upon the heels of *The Youth of Jefferson* with *The Last of the Foresters: or, Humors on the Border; a story of the Old Virginia Frontier*, the third novel to be written in 1854. He "commenced in June or July, stopped at the 5 or 600th page about Aug. 15" to go to the Valley for a six weeks' vacation, returned about the first of October, and finished the work on the seventeenth. The manuscript was at first called *The History of Verty: his performances and pedigree*. The Harpers wisely refused it; but Derby and Jackson accepted it, and advertised it as *Redbud's Necklace*. Either of these titles would have given a suggestion of the nature of the book; but the author and the publisher must have felt that the contents would not bear divulging, for it appeared as *The Last of the Foresters*, a title scarcely applicable, since of the numerous characters the only ones who could possibly be called foresters are an old Indian woman who figures but slightly, and her supposed son, the hero, whose only ''forester''

attributes are an excessive imperviousness to knowledge
and an ability to shoot well. The unfitness of the eleventh
hour title is also patent in the light of historical fact. The
scene is laid in Colonial times, and foresters surely were
not by that time reduced in number to one mild specimen.
The book is a rather unsatisfactory performance. Although it is far better than *Leather Stocking and Silk* in
plot construction, and gives some passably good pictures
of Valley life, it is rendered disagreeable by a very maudlin
love affair. Cooke seems to have thought, for the time at
least, that in composing the new work he was making great
progress stylistically; he referred to the chapter entitled
"The Rose of Glengary" as his "crack writing." The
style of the book is characteristic of the author's more
subjective vein and is commendable; but its gracefulness
and limpidity are not able to counteract the effect of an un-
ending redundancy. Verty, to whom the epithet "dreamy"
is applied literally scores of times, is in love with Squire
Summers's daughter, Redbud, a heroine of the type of Clare
Lee. Redbud—who is soft, sweet, tender, and blushing
throughout—falls into a stream, as do so many of Cooke's
ladies, and takes a terrible cold. She is immature as well
as delicate, for she is only about sixteen and a half years
old when the novel closes. Needless to say the Squire's
daughter cannot marry the fatherless son of the queer Indian woman; consequently, by the frequent transfer of a
necklace and by a birthmark, Verty is discovered to be the
son of a lawyer who has often been sobbing before a portrait of his little child Anna, supposedly a girl. How?
Why, Arthur Anne Rushton is Verty's true designation,
and, as a baby, he was called by a variant of his middle
name!

Throughout *The Last of the Foresters* Cooke revels in
the fine autumn scenery of the Valley, "the loveliness of

the fair fields," "the morning splendors and magnificent
sunsets." "It is in the middle of these scenes that he has
endeavored to place a young hunter—a child of the woods—
and to show how his wild nature was impressed by the new
life and advancing civilization around him. The process
of his mental development is the chief aim of the book."
Verty's progress is disappointing. He changes his clothes
and secures the undesired affection of a spinster boarding-
school mistress, but the Cooperesque "anan," by which he
requests a monosyllabic version of an uncomprehended sentence, is still used on page 393 of a book of 419 pages.
Nothing complimentary can be said of the central romance,
but the Ashley-Fanny, Jinks-Sallianna, Roundjacket-La-
vinia approaches and understandings are by no means disagreeable. They save the novel from being a welter of
insipid sentimentalism. Modern writers have brought in
with the strong man a strong woman, who harks back physically to the vigorous Griselda, but Cooke always shared
the medieval-born admiration of the frail woman. Could
the girl who caught cold at a mere foot-wetting really have
been so attractive? Why should not Mrs. O'Calligan,
"young and handsome, strong and healthy," have been
given at least a chance of being a subsidiary heroine? As
the third book written in a very busy year, *The Last of the
Foresters* was probably an indiscretion of a tired author
who was never at all capable of self-criticism, and whose
friends were in this respect worse than useless since they
would praise anything he showed them. As a motto for
the novel, Cooke chose some lines from *A Midsummer
Night's Dream*. "This weak and idle theme . . . gentles,
do not reprehend," he asks. Surely the kindest criticism
applicable to *The Last of the Foresters* would be that made
by the Hartford *Christian Secretary* of Simms's pseudonymous *Vasconselos*, a criticism which Redfield artlessly

printed in an advertisement of the book: "to such as are fond of this order of literature, it will be found intensely interesting."

As has been shown in the case of *The Knight of Espalion, Evan of Foix,* and *Fairfax,* the order of publication of Cooke's works often differed from that of their composition. In the Spring of 1855 he wrote a book called *Ellie,* which was promptly accepted by the Richmond publisher, A. Morris. Cooke then went on a visit to Amelia County and upon his return to Richmond was told by Morris that Derby and Jackson were about to bring out ahead of *The Last of the Foresters* a work which had been accepted later. The author became angry and wrote at once demanding the return of his manuscript. Derby sent it back. "His note," says Cooke, "was that of a gentleman and I was horrified at what I had so hastily done." To a note of apology Derby replied that, while he might yet bring out the book when times improved, he was perfectly willing for the author to be on the lookout for another publisher. *The Last of the Foresters* appeared in a very attractive form in 1856 under the Derby and Jackson imprint, but the author's ill-advised impulsiveness gave the later-written *Ellie* a priority in publication.

On the title-page of *Ellie: or, the Human Comedy,* John Esten Cooke is described as "author of 'The Virginia Comedians,' 'Leather Stocking and Silk,' 'The Youth of Jefferson,' 'Peony,' etc." "Peony," here included with his three books, was the first *Messenger* article for which the author was paid; it was a purpose story which appeared in the May number of 1852. Its full title was "Peony: a Tale for the Times. Addressed to the Friends and Opponents of Free Schools." The name of the story is taken from Peony, a child who comes "down from the Blue Ridge merrily singing," but is ragged, dirty, and ignorant, and lives amid

squalid surroundings with a drunken father. Presently
everything is shown in a new light: "And Peony had
caused this change throughout! Undoubtedly she had!
She had lent an attentive ear to the Master's directions
(that worthy master who saw all), and gradually the place
became changed. The house was neat: the ground annexed
to it was better tilled: the father had given up his bottle
gradually, and at last wholly: a newspaper, borrowed by
Peony, might often be seen upon the rude but neat pine
table, or in Peony's hands at evening, when all—grouped
around her—listened. The whole was changed, and Peony
had done all—a little child but strong in faith and hope.
. . . Peony changed all—but the FREE SCHOOL changed,
in all things, Peony. They were two different persons, were
they not—the Peony who shook with mirth at a little animal's suffering, and begged in beggar garb upon the high-
way, and that Peony who, snatched from IGNORANCE
and vice, taught her old father there in the glad morning
light?''

"Peony" is a piece of social propaganda which probably
was the germ of *Ellie*. Cooke was profoundly grieved by
his father's death which occurred on December 15, 1854;
and his sorrow, together with his religious awakening earlier
in the year, doubtless prompted a weighing of values, a
search for the why of poverty, and a sounding of the shal-
lowness of the so-called genteel life about him. *Ellie* is in
essence a transcript of Richmond[1] life in the mid-fifties;
but Cooke expressly states that, in drawing his characters,
he had no real persons in mind. For the first time he chose
many of his personages from a sordid milieu. "Why should

[1] Cooke does not localize his story, but references to the river south
of the city, etc., indicate that he had Richmond in mind as the scene
of his events. The society which he knew was, of course, Richmond
society.

our attention be confined to the beautiful flowers, and the noble and straight trees, to the exclusion of the weeds and stunted undergrowth? All is human, and why not look at them, and weigh them?'' Nevertheless, Cooke felt a certain hesitation in depicting low types, and saw fit to explain in his ''Introductory'' that each of his evil characters was neutralized by a good one.

The 576 pages of *Ellie* were reeled off between March 5 and April 6. ''Ellie will create a great talk,'' thought the author, but he was doomed to disappointment. *The Last of the Foresters* retained suggestions of *The Virginia Comedians*. The new book was, on the contrary, completely of the mid-nineteenth century type which depicts the patiently endured sorrow of penniless Christian childhood. *Ellie* is hardly notable in any respect except for the rapidity of its composition, but it is in one key, and avoids the repetitions and the love-drivel of *The Last of the Foresters*. The titular heroine is a little city waif. She and a small brother are brought to extreme poverty by the protracted illness and death of the adults of the family. She receives kindnesses at the hands of a German grocer and a lovable old colored woman, and is befriended by Sansoucy, the genial forward-looking editor of the ''Weekly Mammoth.'' With Ellie and her friend, Lucia, and the latter's boy helper and sweetheart, Wide-awake, as foils, Cooke reviews and satirizes the frivolous elements of society. Miss Incledon is a selfish, unprincipled, ''fast'' young woman of fashion. Fantish is a low-minded, mischief-making dandy who practices on her gullibility and boasts of his familiarity with her. Even more scurrilous than he, is his friend Captain Tarnish. There is a fop, Heartsease, and a Miss Gossyp for him to marry; just as a gracious Miss Aurelia is provided for Sansoucy. The latter and the gruff, good Dr. Fossyl—who suggests Rushton, the rough but kindly lawyer in *The Last*

of the Foresters—are both fond of moralizing, and the book
is replete with disquisitions on such mid-century topics as
the wrong of duelling, the immorality of the newly popu-
larized waltz, and the doubtful utility of "tracts alone when
those for whom they are intended suffer from want of
bread." Ellie, in her rôle of heroine, must of course receive a special dispensation, and at the end she is awarded
the position of long-lost little sister of good Mr. Sansoucy.
In his attack on certain social ills as well as in his depiction of Ellie, Cooke was influenced in a general way by
Dickens. The novel may, in a last analysis, be best described, however, as a very lengthy tract—and an excellent
one.

Cooke's books had up to this time been without pictures,
but David Strother consented to illustrate *Ellie*. He said
that, while he followed his instructions closely, he could
have done better if he had had time to read the manuscript.
He warned the author that it would take about six weeks to
have the engraving well done. "I might have divided the
work and had it done sooner, but Edmonds is the only tolerably reliable cutter of faces and expression that I know,
and he is not above mediocrity. Our American engravers
are no artists as the French are, but simply mechanics and
very dull ones at that. I have prepared the title page for
printing in tints as you ordered." Cooke kept no account of
the financial return from his first few books, but he recorded
that Morris paid for the illustrations of *Ellie* and agreed
to give him ten per cent on all sales.

During the summer of 1855, Cooke apparently developed
a rather serious liking for a young lady of Amelia County.
In his journal he had often set down genial flippant accounts of his "flirting," his "playing second fiddle decidedly," or his finding "one very sweet" girl in every
group. The accounts were little more than the record of

a wholesome and chivalric interest in the young ladies of his acquaintance. After his visit to Amelia in May, however, such notes as he made assumed a decidedly different tone. He now wrote often of a prospective "change" in his life and of a coming "event." Several pages of his journal, in the place where the entries would naturally have been most pertinent, have been torn out, while on the narrow stub in Cooke's handwriting is the comment: "nothing on this." The numerous manuscript poems of this period are very amorous. "Forgotten who and when it was," says a note inscribed beside one of the stanzas in 1867, the year of the author's eventual marriage. The ill-omened love-affair occupied Cooke's mind for at least three years. In March, 1857, he contemplated marriage the following summer. The matter was the subject of serious correspondence with his brothers, but the name of the lady is nowhere mentioned. "I find my affection decreasing for her, I fear," he wrote to "Sainty" in June, 1858. "Well, if she casts it away, my conscience will be clear."

The mental preoccupation attendant upon this cautiously recorded or carefully censored love-affair may have caused Cooke to hesitate to begin a work requiring the steady application which he gave to his novels. However this may be, his next book, *Henry St. John*, was not begun until January, 1856, and was not in the hands of the publishers until early in 1857. Meanwhile he was devoting himself assiduously to the production of magazine articles, and was becoming a figure of national importance. Besides several pieces in the *Messenger*, and such ephemeral work as he was doing for newspapers, Cooke in the year 1856 had five considerable prose articles in *Putnam's Monthly* and four in *Harper's*. The titles are interesting: "In Memoriam," "How I Courted Lulu. In Seven Tableaux," "Annie at the Corner: The History of a Heart," "News from Grassland. A Mountain Letter from John St. John, Esq., to his friend in Town," "John Randolph: A Personal Sketch," "The Tragedy of Hairston," "Baby Bertie's Christmas," "How I was Discarded: By a Married Man," "Fanny and Myself: Being the Recollections of an Elderly Gentleman." A typical early nineteenth century fondness for anonymity and pseudonymity is here displayed; of nine articles six are unsigned, while the other three purport to emanate from three distinct sources. The varied titles show Cooke's wide range of interest, but on close reading almost all the articles prove to be either forerunners or else by-products of his novels or histories. "Baby Bertie's Christmas" is, for instance, very closely akin to "Peony" and *Ellie;* and John Randolph is the subject of a chapter in *Stories of the Old Dominion.*

The novel which Cooke wrote in 1856 was, while in manuscript, successively referred to as a "sequel" to *The Virginia Comedians, Old Virginia,* and *Bonnybel Vane.* The latter name was adopted for a post-bellum reprint, but the Harpers issued the book in 1859 under the designedly old-fashioned title, *Henry St. John, Gentleman, of "Flower of Hundreds," in the County of Prince George, Virginia. A Tale of 1774-'75.* In historic time this sequel follows *The Virginia Comedians* at about a decade. Except for a few vacancies caused by deaths, the characters of the former work are found in the new story. Champ and Will Effingham, Captain Ralph, Lanky Lugg, and their wives, Mr. Crow, Mr. A. Z. Smith, Parson Tag, and others are glimpsed in passing. One or two personages from *The Youth of Jefferson* also make a brief bow. The major plot deals with the love, estrangement, reconciliation and marriage of Bonnybel Vane, the seventeen-year-old daughter of Colonel Vane of Vanely, and Henry St. John, the young master of that famous old estate which was later to be the scene of Mrs. Burton Harrison's *Flower de Hundred*. St. John is a lieutenant in Governor Dunmore's guards, but resigns a position which becomes intolerable. He is succeeded by Lindon who has squandered the greater part of a large estate and desires to stave off creditors by securing the prospective inheritance of Colonel Vane. To break up the correspondence of the lovers, Lindon employs a Miss Carne, a seamstress who is a clever insinuator and a skilful forger. Miss Carne is successful in her mission, but the assiduous Lindon is decidedly unwelcome when he appears as a substitute lover, resuming a repulsed courtship of some time agone. Following the tactics of Effingham, he kidnaps Bonny and is in the preliminaries of a forced marriage when a rescue is effected by St. John, who has been informed by the unpaid and maltreated Miss Carne.

The primary romance is accompanied by the usual quota of subsidiary affairs; but the love interest is less dominant than in the earlier books of the trilogy. ''For the volume has two themes, two aims: the story of a man and a woman; the history, also, of a period in the annals of a nation.'' Charles Waters, since the death of Beatrice, has been working zealously for a republic. Pages are devoted to his political pronouncements. He is no longer merely a bright young liberal alertly interested in governmental topics. He is represented as being the brain, as Henry was the tongue, Jefferson the pen, and Washington the sword of the Revolution. This perversion of historical fact is one of the chief faults of a book which is in most respects a worthy sequel to *The Virginia Comedians*. The portrayal of Dunmore and his entourage is brilliantly done; there is true splendor in the depiction of the last stand of the arrogant alien Governor of Virginia. Cooke on the whole builds rather largely on facts, always of course handling them freely, but sometimes in too much detail, as when he chronicles the

reaction of a dozen counties to the governor's famous removal of the powder. History writing has been placed upon
an entirely different plane since the youth of Cooke, who
in some respects anticipated the modern historian. Like
J. R. Green and later writers he thoroughly realized the
one-sidedness of the traditional war-recording chronicle
which gave rise to the proverb about the blessedness of the
nation without a history. In the quasi-author's prologue
he stated his purpose:

"Where are the men and manners of the Revolution, only hinted
at obscurely in what the world calls histories? Do they exist for
us today except as names and traditions? And what does the present
generation know of them?

"Alas for the historians! They tell us many things, but so little!
They relate, with much dignity, how the battle was fought and the
treaty made—they tell us the number of the combatants, and spread
every protocol upon the page. But the student of the past asks for
more. Of the historian we ask a picture of the older day—portraits
of the Virginian and his household. We would know the peculiari-
ties of character and manner which marked a great race—the worthies of Virginia. We would live again, for a time, beneath those fair
or storm-convulsed skies of 'Old Virginia'; we would take the hand
of the honest old planter; we would go into his library and look
over his shoulder as he reads the new Act in the *Virginia Gazette*,
and would not disdain to scan critically the powdered curls and
looped-back gowns, the flounces, and furbelows, and fancies of the
dames.

"We would see the rude Old-Field School on the edge of the forest,
and listen to the words, and watch the bright faces of these children
who will make hardy patriots and devoted women."

In this late Colonial trilogy—the two parts of *The Virginia Comedians*, and *Henry St. John*—Cooke achieved the
finest product of his career. He attained his difficult goal.
He accomplished the imaginative reconstruction of the life
of a past period with sufficient charm and power almost to
warrant his being called a great social historian. No one

has compressed better than he into three small paragraphs a summary of the third quarter of the eighteenth century in Virginia, a period fascinatingly depicted in this idyllic epic in prose. The quotation is from the Appleton (1883) edition of *The Virginia Comedians:*

"It was the period of the culmination of the old social *régime.* A splendid society had burst into flower, and was enjoying itself in the sunshine and under the blue skies of the most beautiful of lands. The chill winds of the Revolution were about to blow, but no one suspected it. Life was easy, and full of laughter—of cordial greetings, grand assemblies, and the zest of existence which springs from the absence of care. Social intercourse was the joy of the epoch, and crowds flocked to the race-course, where the good horses were running for the cup, or to the cock-fight, where the favorite spangles fought to the death. The violins seemed to be ever playing —at the Raleigh Tavern, in Williamsburg where young Jefferson 'danced with Belinda in the Apollo,' and was happy; or in the great manor houses of the planters clustering along the lowland rivers. In town and country life was a pageant. His Excellency the royal Governor went in his coach-and-six to open the Burgesses. The youths in embroidered waistcoats made love to the little beauties in curls and roses. The 'Apollo' rang with music, the theatre on Gloucester Street with thunders of applause; and the houses of the planters were as full of rejoicing. At Christmas—at every season, indeed—the hospitable old 'nabob' entertained throngs of guests; and, if we choose to go back in fancy, we may see those Virginians of the old age amid their most characteristic surround-ings. The broad board is spread with plenty; the wood fires roar in the fireplaces; the canary sparkles; the wax-lights flame, lighting up the Louis Quatorze chairs, the old portraits, the curious *bric-à-brac,* and the rich dresses of fair dames and gallant men. Care stands out of the sunshine of this brilliant throng, who roll in their chariots, dance the minuet, exchange compliments, and snatch the charm of the flying hours with no thought, one would say, but enjoyment, and to make the best of the little life we live below.

"This is what may be seen on the surface of society under the Old Virginia *régime;* but that social organization had reached a stage when the elements of disintegration had already begun their work. A vague unrest pervaded the atmosphere, and gave warning of the approaching cataclysm. Class distinctions had been immemorially looked upon as a part of the order of nature; but certain curious and restive minds began to ask if that is just, and to glance sidewise at the wealthy nabob in his fine coach. The English Church was the church of the gentry; it was not the church of the people. The 'New Light' ministers began to talk about 'sinegogues of Satan' and to tell the multitudes, who thronged to hear them preach in the fields, that the reverend parsons were no better than they should be. New ideas were on the march. The spirit of change was under the calm surface. The political agitation soon to burst forth was preceded by the social. The hour was near when the merry violins were to stop playing; when the 'Apollo room' at the Raleigh would become the meeting-place of political conspirators; and the Virginians, waking from their dreams of enjoyment, were to be confronted by the hard realities of the new time.

"Such was the period selected by the youthful writer of this volume for the picture he wished to attempt of that former society. When the story opens, the worthy 'Virginia Comedians' have prospered. They have gone away, but have returned year after year, and are still playing at what is now the 'Old theatre near the Capitol.' The winter still attracts the pleasure-loving Virginians to the viceregal city, and throughout the theatrical season, beginning in the autumn, the playhouse is thronged with powdered planters, beautiful dames, honest yeomen, and indented servants. More than ever the spirit of unrest—social, political and religious—pervades all these classes. Revolution is already in the air, and the radical sentiments of young Waters and the man in the Red Cloak, in this volume, meet with thousands of sympathizers. On the surface the era is tranquil, but beneath is the volcano. Passion smoulders under the laughter; the homespun coat jostles the embroidered costume; men are demanding social equality, as they will soon demand a republic; and the splendid old *régime* is about to vanish in the storm of the Revolution."

In the years 1858, 1859, and 1860 Cooke kept no record of any kind. This period was perhaps the least happy of his life. He not only had the grief of his ill-fated love affair, but his spirit had been weighed down by an almost endless chain of deaths. Those of his dearest boyhood friend, his eldest brother, his mother, and his father have been recorded. He had been especially pained by the death of his father who had not been a church member. In 1858, however, in writing to "Sainty" a congratulation upon an expressed determination to become a Christian, Cooke, having examined his father's effects, was able to say: "I found among his papers the most irresistible evidence that he had long been a true believer in Christ. And our dear mother I know has, long since, been reunited to him—she waits for us. I do not believe that God will let *one* of us fail." The grief assuaged by the thought here expressed must soon have descended again upon Cooke with renewed fury, for in little more than a year "Sainty" himself—beloved as the youngest brother and believed to be the most talented member of the family—was dead, and Henry soon followed him to the grave.

The best picture of the young novelist in 1858-59 is given by an admiring friend, George Cary Eggleston, in his *Recollections of a Varied Life*. After discussing "George Prince Regent" James and John Reuben Thompson, Eggleston refers to Cooke as "chief among the literary men of Richmond" and continues:

"The matter of getting a living was a difficult one to him then, for the reason that with a pride of race which some might think quixotic, he had burdened his young life with heavy obligations not his own. His father had died leaving debts that his estate could not pay. As the younger man got nothing by inheritance, except the traditions of honor that belonged to his race, he was under no kind of obligation with respect to those debts. But with a chivalric loyalty such as few men have ever shown, John Esten Cooke made his dead father's debts his own and little by little discharged them with the earnings of a toilsome literary activity.

"His pride was so sensitive that he would accept no help in this, though friends earnestly pressed loans upon him when he had a payment to meet and his purse was well-nigh empty. At such times he sometimes made his dinner on crackers and tea for many days together, although he knew he would be a more than welcome guest at the lavish tables of his many friends in Richmond. It was a point of honor with him never to accept a dinner or other invitation when he was financially unable to dine abundantly at his own expense."

During this period of grief, hard work, and high idealism Cooke was, as he recalled years later, doing "editorial matter" which "amounted to very considerable" in the "*Messenger, Express, Index, Whig,* etc., etc.*" He wrote a number of articles for Appleton's *Cyclopædia,* and continued his contributions to magazines. For the latter he seems at this time to have been paid a normal maximum of seventy-five dollars per article. Such work afforded money certainly more promptly, and probably in larger amounts than could be secured from the royalties of a slow-selling book. Whether Cooke desired the cash in hand which a serial was supposed to fetch, or whether, more probably, he sought a publisher in vain, the longer stories written in the years 1857-1860 all appeared as serials. *Estcourt* "was written in 1857 at the request of Paul Hayne and appeared in *Russell's Magazine."* "I have always liked it," Cooke wrote later, "Was paid $50, leaving $250 due—which Paul offered me his poor little copyright on *Avolio* for—and I 'indignantly refused.' ''[1] Of the composition of *Falkland* and *The Shadow on the Wall,* Cooke in his post-bellum literary reminiscences says nothing except that they appeared in small-town newspapers, and served, both of them, as a basis for a later novel, *Dr. Vandyke.* These stories were probably written some time in 1858 or 1859, for another work, *The Pride of Falling Water,* occupied

[1] In a letter to Cooke, Hayne expressed bitter regret at this inability to pay.

Cooke in the spring of 1860. Crushed by grief, he felt "exceedingly weak and sick," and only his "word pledged to the *Field and Fireside* editor" drove him "to the pen." For this serial he received three hundred dollars, and a similar sum was brought by a "remoulded" version which he published in the St. Louis *Home Journal* in 1872-73 as *Paul, the Hunter.*

In the large amount of prose which Cooke produced in the closing fifties his work for Appleton's *New American Cyclopædia* is perhaps most worthy of note. The encyclopedia was edited jointly by George Ripley and Charles A. Dana, both of whom wrote often to Cooke. "I am," said Ripley in one of his letters, "perfectly aware of the onerous nature of the task; but with the large circulation of the N. A. C. and the national character, which we mean to give it *à tout prix*, I am sure you will find some relish in increase of fame, and in your close identification with the first attempt, on so large a scale, to do ample honor to the illustrious sons of your ancestral soil." After a few of Cooke's contributions had been received, Ripley wrote as follows: "We are highly gratified with the spirit, ability, and artistic grace of your biographical sketches, and earnestly hope that you will be able to furnish us with many other of the eminent statesman [*sic*] of Virginia. Should also any name, outside that category, in American or English Literature occur to you as a favorite subject, we shall be happy to receive it from your pen." Among Cooke's numerous articles were sketches of Madison, Monroe, and Marshall, and of four members of the Lee family. The invitation to write the paper on Irving was a very particular compliment to Cooke's tact as well as his ability, for Irving was not only still alive but, because of his distinguished public service and his priority to the great New England writers,

was an exceedingly lofty figure. "Admirable" is the word
Dana applied to Cooke's "Irving." Cooke contributed a
long article on Jefferson which Bancroft, who saw it in
manuscript, described to Ripley as "a masterly production,
showing very accurate knowledge of the subject, and open
to but few criticisms." "It is a matter of great importance," Dana had said, "to present the facts, and all the
facts, of his career in a manner which no party, either
Democrats or Federalists, of old, or Democrats and Repub-
licans of our day, can impugn." Cooke succeeded in doing
this, but his paper is open to attack on the ground of faulty
proportion. There is no account at all of Jefferson's later
years; no mention of the founding of the University of Virginia, a work which he commemorated in his epitaph as one
of the three great achievements of his life.

Throughout his career Cooke wrote poetry, and his poems
attracted some attention. He was frequently referred to
as a poet rather than a novelist. His verse was published
in *Harper's*, he was included in the contemporary anthologies, and had been asked by a New York publishing house
to bring out, with Thompson as his collaborator, *The Poets
and Poetry of the South*, a work which was well under way
when the war interrupted it, but was never completed. These
facts would seem to indicate that Cooke had considerable
poetic ability, but such was hardly the case. The mid-
century was not over-critical; a wholesome theme was
nearly all that was demanded. Cooke's rapidity of composition was responsible for his chief shortcomings. His
poems not only frequently lack the fine finish of perfection,
but are sometimes faulty in rime and meter. Such of them
as escape technical carelessness are mildly acceptable, but
few exhibit marked vigor or originality. "Clouds," suggestive of Bryant's "To a Water-fowl" and Whittier's later

"The Eternal Goodness," shows Cooke's faults and some of the beauties which the faults obscure:

CLOUDS

I know not whither past the crimson zone
Of evening sail those ships of snow and gold—
The beauteous clouds that seem to hover and fold
Their wings—like birds that having all day flown
Against the blue sky, now at set of sun
    Play for a moment gayly on their soft
    And burnished pinions wide: then from aloft
Sink down below the horizon and are gone!
I know not where they fold their shining wings
    In very truth; nor what far happy land
    They come together in—a radiant band,
The brightest, purest, of all earthly things!
But well I know that land lies broad and fair
Beyond the evening: oh! that I were there!

"Kane," commemorative of the death of the Arctic explorer, may owe something to Tennyson's "Ode on the Death of the Duke of Wellington." It is an occasional poem of dignity, as may be inferred from the first stanza:

"What plumes are these?
Sad mourners sweeping like the wings of night
Over the dark waves of the wide Balize
Where the great waters sink into the main?
What wail of pain
Strikes the bent ear, what sombre sight;
Looms on the waters, where the ocean breeze
    Ripples the sad, deep seas?"

In "A Dream of the Cavaliers," a poem, over two hundred lines long, which appeared in *Harper's* for January, 1861, Cooke had a subject well suited to his talents:

". . . So I pass to the long-gone summers
    Of the unremembered years,
And share in the joys and sorrows,
    In the April smiles and tears.

"With the Cavaliers and the maidens,
    In an idle smiling dream,
I wander away to the forest,
    Or sail on the rippling stream:

"I hear as I sit and ponder
    On the trellis'd porch of the hall,
The tinkle of fairy laughter
    From under the oak-trees tall:

"And stroll with the bright-eyed damsels,
    As they list to the flattering tale
Told by the gay young gallants,
    In the moonlight weird and pale:

"The Comedy plays before me,
    And there on the shining shore,
With the foolish murmuring lovers,
    I live in the days before!"

The end of 1860 saw the close of Cooke's first phase as a writer. He had been self-supporting and had been of financial aid to several members of his family. His reputation for trustworthy scholarship was confirmed by his being asked to write for Appleton's *Cyclopædia*. He was upon terms of friendly intimacy with Duyckinck, Stedman, and others of the New York literati, and corresponded with still others, including Halleck and Willis. Irving, with whom he spent a summer day in 1859, wrote asking him to come again if he could, as his visit was very refreshing. From his home at Fort Lee on the Palisades, Thomas Dunn English wrote often, and later named a seedling dahlia for his literary friend in the South. Children were named for Cooke, and he received letters from admirers whose "cup of happiness" he would "fill to overflowing" by a reply. He was thanked in a printed memorandum for the "suitable sublime and brilliant" ritual he had prepared for his fraternal order, the Red Men. Most important of all, his shorter articles were appearing in the leading magazines, and his books were being brought out by the best publishing houses in America. Few, if any, of his contemporaries had, at the age of thirty, greater fame than was enjoyed by John Esten Cooke.

Cooke also received his share of critical attention, much of it laudatory, but in this regard he was not unique, as George W. Bagby complains in the Richmond *Whig* for August 9, 1858. Bagby says that all Virginia novelists were praised equally as displaying "genius of no common order," and continues: "No wonder some of them retired in disgust. No wonder that some of them, emulous of the speed of Dumas rather than the patience of Talfourd and the assiduity of Richter, agreed to write a novel in twenty minutes by a stop-watch. No wonder that all of them wrote carelessly. No wonder that all of them at last benevolently wrote no more." The publication of *Henry St. John* was the occasion of another tirade in the *Whig* about a year later. Cooke had been mentioned in the previous article, but the latter, although it takes a passing fling at six others, was actually entitled "Unkind but Complete Destruction of John Esten Cooke, Novelist."

"I now come," says Bagby, "to the most profuse and abandoned novelist of them all, to wit, Effingham Cooke." Bagby examines the book and is "constrained to pronounce it perhaps the most excusable of all his misdemeanors. . . . There is a girl in it who will take all the boys, and a young man who will take all the girls. The pretty pictures of the Colonial times will please the old folks. And the thing will take all around. . . .

"Well, let it take. The unfortunate writer will need all he will make to pay funeral expenses. I am about to demolish him. I shall do so by preferring against him two charges, both entirely true, and of so grave a nature that no man, and particularly no novelist, can live under the weight of them.'' The first of these charges is ''Mr. Cooke's eyes are in the back of his head.'' After scoring the novelist vigorously, Bagby continues: ''I'm proud of my granddaddy, proud of the day and the deeds of his generation; but I don't want to get so plague-taked proud of him and his times as to undervalue myself and my times. The old times may have been mighty good, but there are some first rate days and prime doings left. Therefore I desire that Effingham Cooke shall sell out his old stock, close business in the Behind, and set up in the Now.'' The second charge was: ''Mr. Cooke's eyes are not only in the back of his head, but they are also afflicted with a pair of rose-colored goggles of enormous magnifying powers.'' Bagby dwells again on the glory of the Colonial era as portrayed by Cooke and takes up in detail a typical heroine: ''Is she pretty—I mean Cooke's dead old young female? She is that—prodigiously pretty. Is she delightful, merry, jolly, full of life and fun, coquettish yet true, skittish yet thoroughbred, and all that? She is—you'd better believe she is. . . . And I marvel much that such a set of homely, selfish, money-loving cheats and rascals as we are, should have descended from such remarkably fine parents. No doubt it is very good noveling, but I swear it is wretched physiology.''

Bagby's criticism[1] prompts a general summary of the eight volumes which have been commented on and which formed the bulk of Cooke's ante-bellum work. All eight are novels of Virginia, and they cover three localities and phases of the life of the state. No writer had yet dedicated himself so whole-heartedly to the service of the Old

[1] After the Civil War Bagby himself idealized the old South. See his *Old Virginia Gentleman.*

Dominion. The four volumes dealing with Colonial life in the Tidewater region are on a distinctly higher plane than the others; in them Cooke exhibits a splendid detachment while he weaves into the border romances and *Ellie* a vast amount of personal idiosyncrasy and reminiscence. In discussing Cooke's literary output one should bear in mind the general state of the novel in America in the fifties. Flights in the "grand style," romantic adventure, pathos, sentiment—these were the ingredients, and Cooke abused them no more than most of his contemporaries. If the rosebud maidens are said to be superb and are not shown to be, one must again blame the custom of the period. The modern novel is much closer to the drama. Cooke did not like Dickens, but he outdoes him in repeating favorite words and phrases. Wagner's mustache in *Fairfax* is referred to even oftener than the "post-office" mouth in *Great Expectations*. The marriage of first cousins was much too frequently a feature of upper class life in Virginia, where the estates were so scattered that the only mutually marriageable young persons were likely to be relatives. Nearly all Cooke's leading lovers are first cousins, for instance, Beatrice and Charles in *The Virginia Comedians* and Bonny and St. John in *Henry St. John*. The inbreeding continues in the second generation, when a second generation is portrayed. Thus Max Courtlandt marries his cousin in *Leather Stocking and Silk*, and Max, Junior, also marries his cousin. Cooke, who boasted that his ancestors had not married first cousins, realized the objections to such marriages, but never hinted at them in his books.

Perhaps the best general comment on Cooke's eight years as a writer was pronounced by William Gilmore Simms in a review of *Henry St. John*:

"Mr. Cooke is in possession of admirable material for art, resuscitating the ancient life of the Old Dominion in the days of its grand

and vigorous development. And we repeat, if true to his own genius, no one can surpass him in the happy and noble use of this grand moral material. He has done well, so far; but his sinews must be a little more seasoned by the proper exercise; his mind more patient, more deliberate, more sensible of the burden of the task, more greatly stirred within him, by the hourly growing sense of the value of his theme; so that he shall shape it with proper care, with a becoming purpose, and under a severer, sublimer design."

There is a special significance in the fact that *Henry St. John*, Cooke's last book before the Civil War, portrayed the quiet life of Colonial Virginia with its seething undercurrent which broke to the surface as revolution. In quite a parallel fashion, the author himself was playing a part in the last scene of another phase of Southern society, a scene in which many of the actors were wholly serene and few realized the momentous conflagration that was having its fuel prepared by the bitterness and obstinacy of the two leading national factions. The presidential election of 1860 served, however, to crystallize public sentiment. It made of Cooke an ardent secessionist, and he chafed greatly, as he recounts in his renewed diary, at Virginia's delay in following South Carolina along what he considered to be the path of right and honor.

CHAPTER III

THE CIVIL WAR—SOLDIER AND HISTORIAN

FROM his unchronicled three-year period of depression Cooke's recovery was sudden. His deep personal grief was lost sight of in the intensity of his feeling on national events. He renewed his diary on February 18, 1861, chiefly to record his views on secession, the grave issue then confronting Virginia:

"Here I sit in my little room in the 'little wooden house festooned with roses,' near the Equestrian Washington yonder—just going to Col. Fontaine's to spend the evening with Cousins Kate and Mollie, my little pet Marie S. and Miss Ellen Pollard—here, in February of the year of Revolutions—the same book before me which has recorded ever since 1851 my errant career.

"Here once more—the same, but changed!

"What shall I write? Where shall I begin writing? I cannot think of putting down these years. They are dead—I survive.

"Yet, after all my woes, I still retain at thirty, at least cheerfulness and good spirits. But my light-heartedness is gone.

"The Convention is here; and Wise the 'Old Roman Eagle,' as Dick calls him, has just excoriated Stuart and Moore. Success to him. Take them one by one, my old Roman, and speak for the liberties of Virginia!

"Overton was defeated—Randolph elected—him with whom I made the campaign in the 'Wise War.' We had great times at the City Hall and Lower Ward polls that snowy fourth of February; and between Lewis Randolph and Bob Wms. I nearly had occasion to use my little five shooter.

"Will war come? If it does, and I fall, this page will remain. But I here direct whoever loves me, if they find this volume, to destroy it. 'Tis intended for no eye but mine—Remember!"

Thus Cooke played his wonted part in the life of Richmond and awaited the unrolling of destined events. His daily routine, as recorded in several detailed entries, was much the same as in the middle fifties. The old names of friends recur, and there are new ones. Cooke had often visited at the executive mansion in the days when Wise was governor, and he seems to have been quite an intimate friend of the governor's daughter Annie[1] (later Mrs. Hobson), the novelist and the first young lady of the state each perhaps enjoying the glamor afforded by associating with the other. The governor esteemed Cooke most highly, as Annie informed him, and in 1861 the impatient writer often sought counsel of his old friend. The following is the entry of March 6:

"The year of Revolution."

"We are in the midst of it . . . and yesterday the submissionists in the Convention—Dorman of Rockbridge at least—thought the time had come when every one should stand fast for—the union.

"Low and cowardly submission sounds the deepest depths of infamy. But let it pass. We'll fight, and the time is near.

"Yesterday evening I went to the Ballard House and had a long talk with the old governor. . . .

"I can't compose, I can't think of anything but Virginia's degradation.

"But we'll fight our way out yet, and crush the miserable intriguans [sic] who are stifling the brave old commonwealth—for brave I do believe she is at her heart.

"God defend the right!"

The vehemence with which Cooke embraced the cause of secession does not imply that he did so without a careful balancing of the issues then prominent. Robert E. Lee's reluctance in quitting the United States Army was dwelt upon by Cooke in his life of the General, and is well-known.

[1] The story "Annie at the Corner" is a tribute to Miss Wise. It was printed in *Putnam's Monthly* in June, 1856, and was republished in *Pretty Mrs. Gaston, and Other Stories*, in 1874. Of Mrs. Hobson, Prof. William Peterfield Trent says: "My first teacher, and a charming woman, who must have been very pretty in her youth."

Paul Hamilton Hayne's career closely parallels that of Cooke—both were born in 1830, both died in 1886, and both rendered distinguished service as officers in the Confederate army—yet in May, 1860, Hayne felt so disgusted with the Charleston Convention that he unburdened himself to his Virginia friend: "I must say, that I never saw (of course there were illustrious exceptions), a *dirtier*, a more *blackguard* set of fellows; half of the number were drunk, and the remainder could hardly be called sober. In sad earnest, what, *mon ami*, is to be the fate of this great Republic? Are we not drifting headlong to the Devil?" Cooke, like Hayne, kept an open mind until he felt it necessary to choose definitely one way or the other.

John Esten's soldier uncle, Philip St. George Cooke, who had spent much of his time on the Western frontier, cast his lot with the North and remained an officer in the Union army. "Flora," he had written to his nephew in 1856, "was married, rather suddenly—to Mr. [J. E. B.] Stuart of Va. . . . He is a remarkably fine, promising, pure young man; and has had so far extraordinary promotion. He is a 1st Lieut. 1st Cavalry." This son-in-law and an only son, John Rogers Cooke, II, joined the Southern army upon the outbreak of hostilities. "Those mad boys," the father is reported to have said when called in from the West, "if only I had been here." In the Peninsula battles the Northern general commanded a cavalry division and was opposed by his son-in-law and his nephew—a notable pair, for the son-in-law was the greatest of Confederate cavalrymen, and the nephew was perhaps the best known writer engaged on either side. Just how close he came to his enemy uncle, Cooke of course never knew, but in a Confederate advance he picked up and later preserved in his scrap-book an envelope addressed to him. The Pendletons and Kennedys, and others of Cooke's kin who lived near the upper Potomac, witnessed in their families a division similar to that among the Cookes. Here then was the basis for the pitting of relative against relative —a characteristic of the plot of each of Cooke's Civil War romances, and of nearly all later stories of the Civil War.

Cooke's military career really began before the Civil War. He joined the Richmond Howitzers, apparently in the late fifties, and was despatched to Harper's Ferry upon the occasion of the John Brown raid. At the beginning of the war, the company of Howitzers was expanded to a battalion and Cooke was made a sergeant, in which capacity he commanded a gun at First Manassas. "He was powder-blackened," wrote George Cary Eggleston, who chanced to see him on the field of battle, "and he had lost both his coat and his hat in the eagerness of his service at the piece; but during a brief pause in the firing he greeted me with a rammer in his hand and all the old cheeriness in his face and voice." Cooke was soon a first lieutenant, was recommended for a captaincy, and was sent to Richmond in 1862 to recruit a company for the Horse Artillery. Whether or not success was achieved by his advertisement in a paper and by his poster headed "100 Patriotic Men Wanted," he does not say, but by March he was chafing terribly under the inaction. "My valley," he wrote, "my cousins, nieces, and the graves of my brothers are in possession of a brutal and infamous foe. Banks is ere now master of Winchester." Cooke describes a splendid review of Stuart's cavalry on Franklin Street. The youthful general is ready for Cooke as soon as he is commissioned. "My whole heart goes out to that gallant defender of our liberties . . . if I can only get my commission and be sent to Yorktown where there is imminent danger of a fight—this may be the last entry in this book I will ever make—if I fall the enemy will have stilled a heart as true as any that beats, to the Southern land." He speaks of the likelihood of being detailed as a private for some local police-work. "So be it," he concludes. "Any capacity that helps the cause suits me."

Cooke was soon again to see active service with Stuart in the famous ride around McClellan. "It was a splendid affair," he recorded on June 16, "and Stuart is the king of the hour. . . . I will only say that I was busy all the expedition: carrying orders up and down the line everywhere—and that Gen. Jeb. (in the words of the 'Dispatch') seemed 'pleased' with me. I don't care whether he was or not—I know I did the best I could, and on the chicken hominy, as Captain Von Borcke calls it, I laughed and joked, and cheered the men, when the river was in front and—Gen. Cooke in the rear! They sent for him I heard, and Stuart escaped him. Stuart must be a great general to foil his father-in-law. . . . I think Gen. Cooke a man of first rate military genius. Why did not he *follow the hoof marks on a dirt road of 2000 cavalry?* Perhaps what Mrs. Morris says is true—that he is perfectly miserable and hopes the first ball will kill him. Sad, very sad. . . . Well, here I am where I never expected to be. I doubted if I would arrive. . . . Gen. Jeb. is a trump, and I am tired and sleepy. 25 times asleep in the saddle."

Cooke seems to have served continuously in the defense of the capital against McClellan. In the middle of July he was in Richmond, "home again after Cold Harbor, the White House, and Charles City," was "sick and languid from bile caught in the White Oak Swamp," and was chafing at the army's failure to assume a constant offensive. "If I get thro' this war I will have much to write of—if. My notes of the great trip with Jackson's army to Cold Harbor and back, are in my little book[1] which I carry in

[1] The loss of this diary left the first two years of Cooke's war service largely unrecorded.

my breast pocket—written on the field and fresh with the spirit of the moment. . . . The war groes [sic] tiresome —very. When will it end? The lying Northern prints prolong it—following the beck of a bestial, foul-souled administration. I see but one hope of a speedy end to it—the English fleet. But to that we should not, and will not look.''

Perhaps on the basis of his participation in Stuart's ride, Cooke received his regular commission as Captain of Artillery in July, 1862. ''Here I am,'' he wrote in Richmond on August 17, ''smoking in my room, on Sunday evening— having been sent down by mon genèral [sic] on Ordnance business. I have gone up with him one step—being now 'Captain of Artillery,' and 'Ord. Off. Stuart's Cav. Divn.' Another bar upon the collar and the cuff—and some more satisfaction. My boy[1] is safe again after 'Cedar Run.' But poor Dick Cunningham is gone—my old friend and comrade. God rest him! This book will go under lock and key directly; so—we are on the march to take the front of Jackson's army, which will press the vulgar bully Pope to the wall. Then, ho! for Maryland and Pennsylvania. The war grows more desperate with every battle—and must soon end. God grant it. For me, I am agreeably fixed with Stuart; some fine fellows on the staff—some very poor company—and I like my life; making myself busy and useful. I dream, between times, of happier times, of tranquil country haunts, of writing, pondering on those times with Nat and my dear ones around me. May God the all Merciful preserve my boy and all my dear ones, and me— but more than our lives, our souls. To Him, be glory and praise and submission. Still: Esperance! Toujours.''

After about a year's service as captain, part of the time

[1] Philip Pendleton Cooke's eldest son, Nathaniel, often referred to as Nat.

as aide-de-camp to Stuart, Cooke had, in the words of his friend Eggleston, earned a reputation for "nonchalance under fire" and an "eager readiness to undertake Stuart's most perilous missions," and was recommended by the great cavalryman as a major for his staff with transfer from artillery to ordnance. Eggleston gives a delightful account of the dramatic way in which Stuart chose to break the news to Cooke:

"'You're about my size, Cooke,' Stuart said, 'but you're not so broad in the chest.'

"'Yes, I am,' answered Cooke.

"'Let's see if you are,' said Stuart, taking off his coat as if stripping for a boxing match. 'Try that on.'

"Cooke donned the coat with its three stars on the collar, and found it a fit.

"'Cut off two of the stars,' commanded Stuart, 'and wear the coat to Richmond. Tell the people in the War Department to make you a major and send you back in a hurry. I'll need you tomorrow.'"

This promotion was approved by Lee who at once began to call Cooke Major, a title bestowed upon him throughout the remainder of his life by his comrades in arms. General Cooper of the Richmond staff ruled, however, that Stuart already had his full complement of majors, but gave Cooke a temporary transfer to the Ordnance Department. Lieutenants Freanor and Ryals and Captain White of Stuart's division were soon advanced over Cooke, and he entered a protest. He was a personal friend of the three officers, was not jealous of their promotion, but wished if possible to remove the reflection on his ability as an officer occasioned thereby. Although making no formal complaint, he urged that something be done. But Lee, Stuart, and his own efforts could not avail. He was still a captain at the end of the war.

Cooke was permanently grieved by this failure to advance in grade and never understood why he was not promoted.

He preserved all the documents in the case to show the high quality of his recommendations. The secret of the matter seems to lie in certain eventualities that grew out of his being a man of letters. The *Life of Stonewall Jackson,* which appeared soon after the general's death in 1863, contains quietly worded passages which might well have nettled a high-handed and inexperienced administration. Cooke, like Jackson, was unalterably of the party which pleaded for a policy of following up successes with the view of destroying the retreating army. The aim of the staff at the capital seemed to him less the winning of the war than the protection of Richmond. Cooke had also been a leading contributor to the *Messenger,* and the *Messenger* was constantly flaying the administration. Besides the *Life of Jackson,* which was really only an account of Jackson's battles, he wrote poems and long dispatches for the Richmond papers. His maps of battles made their way into the press. In his "Outlines from the Outpost," in the *Southern Illustrated News,* Cooke spoke in superlative terms of the Stonewall Brigade. This was not always appreciated—elicited, in fact, expressions of disapproval from excited readers. "I see no reason," wrote one, "why the Army of the Potomac, except the *Stonewall Brigade,* should not be disbanded and sent home, and leave that *immortal Brigade* which has done all the fighting to crown themselves with immortality by ending the war alone." An illiterate private, or more probably someone posing as such, wrote: "the Solgars is hard down on that artical tell that Riter fo God Sak to stop it." In the case of Cooke, the writer was, thus, never fully submerged in the soldier, and the writer always said what he thought or wished to say. To deny promotion upon such grounds, is natural, if not noble; but Cooke was too high-souled to suspect the apparent reason for his having never obtained his majority.

Cooke's numerous staff duties caused him to see much of the generals of the Army of Northern Virginia. He narrates some interesting anecdotes. "Gen. Early and Gov. Letcher lived with us. Early a gay old *militaire:* he and the Gov. running each other incessantly." Stuart was famous for his liking for music. He recruited his band from the best talent of his command—in at least one case to the great displeasure of Colonel, later Brigadier-General, Thomas T. Munford.[1] While Cooke wrote in his tent on army and personal matters the great cavalryman would often be singing "Her bright smile haunts me still," or other favorite songs. High officers were sometimes flippant. Gordon severely teased Venable in a "discussion of the propriety or impropriety of kissing—Gordon urging former with a side wink" at Cooke, while Venable remained "horrorstruck and indignantly virtuous." In the case of the enemy, jokes were sometimes replaced by potentially serious moves. Having captured a Federal officer's trunk containing beautiful letters from a wife and obscene ones from a mistress reveling in the wife's ignorance of the relation, Stuart sent all of them to the wife, Cooke inferring, doubtless correctly, that there would be a "fuss in that family." But "Yankee" officers were not always sordid. Philip Pendleton Cooke's daughters were in occupied territory and "a Yankee Lieut." brought to

---

[1] "The Sweeneys, two quite celebrated minstrels, had enlisted in the Appomattox Company of my Regt.; they were great banjo and violinists, and General Stuart's feet would shuffle at their presence or naming. He issued an order for them to report at his quarters and 'detained them.' It was a right he enjoyed, but not very pleasing to me or my Regiment. 'Music hath charms to soothe the savage breast.' When Capt. Cooke was on Stuart's staff he used to laugh at me for 'not coming over to enjoy our music,' until it came to be a sore subject to me."—General Munford to J. O. B., January 14, 1917.

Pennie with his compliments a copy of the New York edition of her uncle's *Life of Stonewall Jackson*. ''On the road to the second Manassas,'' Cooke saw Lee, who as usual impressed him profoundly: ''Gen. Lee's attitude was what I have always seen in him everywhere—one of invincible, supreme repose: and settled resolution—as of a man whom no reverse can dismay, and no anxiety flurry. This, which I have *seen*, a hundred times, convinces me that Lee is, in the foundation of his character, as in the superstructure, a very great man. No man in public affairs now, is so great a type of the great Virginia race. He reminds me always of my father.''

In his various capacities Cooke was often detailed on long journeys, alone or with but few attendants. He enjoyed the chincapins, chestnuts, persimmons, and wild grapes which, in season, abounded in rural Virginia. In all save one or two cases he was fed gladly by those at whose houses he stopped, and often rewarded graciousness by a word in his diary. ''Went with Major Peyton to Mr. Finks' —Bob Hunter and Ben Turner along—and got 'refreshments' liquid and solid. Fell in love with Miss Lucy's lips and dimples—she is very like Pelham. She knew Farley; he had often been there . . . bless her!—also Mrs. Finks. Dimples in former; kindness in latter, overwhelming.'' But Cooke's good words were not spoken of the upper classes only. The possession of social privileges did not make him disagreeable either toward colored persons or toward whites less well situated in the world. Before the war the Cooke family went once, upon invitation, to eat a dinner prepared for them by Mammy Giddy in her Richmond cabin. ''I must speak of Miss Lang,'' says Cooke in his war-diary, describing a hospitable reception on one of his journeys. ''She was a girl of sixteen or seventeen apparently, of the poorer class. . . . She . . . had the softest, sweetest voice I

think I ever heard. She was tolerably good-looking—wore
no hoops—and lent me with a smile Sue's 'Ater Gull' [*sic*],
'Female Bluebeard' and other blood and thunder romances,
picked up from the Yankees.'' He further records that she
attended to his "supper-cravings" with "great good nature,'' and concludes: "May she be happy.'' Cooke not only
supplied himself with personal accessories such as a rain-
coat, a blanket, and a pair of trousers, upon a Federal retreat, but on more than one occasion made additions to his
library. Between his duties and his writing he naturally
had no time for an extended course of reading. In camp,
however, he had a habit of rising early to read chapter after
chapter in the Bible by firelight before taking up the day's
duties, and devoted himself assiduously to such serious
works as Bourrienne's *Memoirs of Napoleon Bonaparte*.

A young lady of Cooke's chance acquaintance urged
him to be sufficiently brave, but not reckless. He may not
have been unduly reckless habitually, but he soon learned
on his rides not to let the enemy hurry him too quickly
from a meal. Once, in Fauquier, he was driven away from
a "party *en règle*—low necks, bare arms, fine dresses,''
by an excited cavalryman who mistakenly supposed the
enemy was approaching. He finally reached the stage where
he would continue to eat from a plate standing by his
horse until a hostile scouting squad was within two hundred
yards, and then toss down his coffee and gallop away.

On Lee's advance into Pennsylvania Cooke's entertain-
ment in Maryland was quite as generous as it was in Virginia, though such was not the fate of the army as a whole.
Maryland youth seemed to be fascinated by the Southern
cause. The Confederate cavalry was given an enthusiastic
reception by the young ladies of the Rockville female seminary who flocked to the windows in holiday costume waving
sheet music bearing Confederate flags. Cooke, however,

met in Maryland one situation which baffled him. When
the Confederates occupied Westminster, he was detailed to
search the house of a Captain Wampler and bring away the
United States Post Office money which was known to be concealed in it. The captain was ostensibly suffering too much
to speak, and his little daughter conducted the unwelcome
visitor through the various rooms. Cooke became very
much ashamed at rummaging among her garments and
trinkets, was sure the man had the money beneath him in
bed, but did not have the heart to move him as he was crying
out in pain with his wife at his side. Cooke said he would
search no more houses if the ladies objected. A feature
of the Northern advance was the purchase of articles at a
reasonable price. In Virginia, after buying the cloth, Cooke
had had to pay $175 for the mere tailoring of a suit; and
at Christmas, 1863, when he went to see his sister Sal he
carried two pounds of candy which had cost $8 a pound.

Many of Cooke's war notes were written in winter quarters in 1863-64 near Orange. He was comfortably established in an abode which he called the ''Wigwam:'' ''My
tent is on the side of the hill, just above the general's and
I have a huge stone fireplace, built by myself, a bed of logs,
plank, and Yankee tick, stuffed with hay—desk here on the
right: plank hearth; saddle on crosspiece in the corner
to my right . . .'' In this retreat he recorded the personal
element in his campaigning, and took stock of his imagined
aging, of his lessening susceptibility to female beauty.
''What ails me. I dream no longer—and 'love' no one—
in the romantic sense. Am I growing cold, as I certainly
am getting old? The gayest eyes do not move Mr. Joyeuse Gent.[1] The other day Marion Skelton who is certainly
a perfect little beauty was so outrageous as to *put her head*

[1] "Tristan Joyeuse, Gent." was a pseudonym under which Cooke
published some of his fugitive ante-bellum work.

on one side, look at me coquettishly, and murmur as the
romance writers say, in a languid tone, with a golden smile,
'you needn't try to resist and stay away—for you'll find
at last, you can't *live without me!*' . . . I could have
kissed the pretty mouth that uttered the words, and was
then so near—but sentiments of propriety forbade. And
the words scarcely moved this old bird of 33.''

Of late '64 and early '65 Cooke had nothing to say. A
crushing sense of the futility of further struggle for the
Southern cause probably descended upon him, just as the
numerous deaths in his family bore down his spirit at the
close of the fifties. He kept no diary; and sisters, nephew,
and nieces complained of not hearing from him for months.
Fighting as he did at First Manassas and surrendering at
Appomattox, Cooke always considered it remarkable that
he never received a wound. In his diary he checked off
his fallen friends and relatives, and recounted his escapes.
Once a bullet struck a fence but a few inches from his head;
again, he was stunned by a bursting shell and was covered
by the thrown-up earth. It was, however, an old habit to
close every entry with an expression of hope in God, and
he saw fulfilled his reiterated wish to be allowed to return
to his beloved Valley. After Stuart's death at Yellow
Tavern, Cooke had been assigned to the staff of General
Pendleton and was his inspector-general of horse artillery
when the end came. Paroled at Appomattox, he is said
to have buried his silver spurs upon the field to avoid de-
livering them to his late foes.

Cooke's parents had never owned a home in Richmond.
They and his brothers were dead, and the city's periodicals
had been wrecked by the war—so Cooke now regarded
Richmond neither as his home nor as a suitable place for
earning a livelihood. . . . One sister lived in Amelia, and
one in New Kent, but the great bulk of his relatives

lived in the neighborhood of Winchester. "My first thought on the surrender," he wrote, "was to go to Amelia—get my two horses fat on grass—sell them—go to N. Y.—write, and look Paris-ward." But the more practical if less imaginative Ned Dandridge said "Come on, let's go home." Cooke and two others joined him, and covered in nine days the distance from Appomattox to the Valley neighborhood where the writer's civilian life was to be renewed among his relatives and amid the scenes of his boyhood.

When Cooke reached the lower valley he stopped at "The Vineyard," the home of the family of his brother Philip, for a month of idleness and rest—needed, one can well imagine, by a veteran of Lee's army. During the summer he made several visits, but in the fall settled definitely at "The Vineyard." Since Cooke had owned no real estate, the end of the war had left him absolutely penniless. He was not, however, without potential assets. He had an enlarged life of Jackson in manuscript; he had, of course, his reputation as a writer; and he had a vast unworked field to draw upon for subject-matter. His military duties and achievements; his acquaintance with the great Confederate leaders while they were in action; his diary-chronicled adventures of securing food, seeing pretty women, and escaping death—these were not the only features of Cooke's four years of war. He had carried into his experiences a romantic turn of mind, and in every lurking figure saw—at least in retrospect—not only a wary spy, but a person on sinister private business. Remote places were easily peopled in his imagination by characters intent upon crime, or escape, or vengeance.

Cooke's material for writing was thus of a threefold nature. He might devote himself to the history of the period, he might record anecdotes and personal reminiscences, or he might use his experience as the basis of fiction. In fact,

he used the same material in all three ways. His writings
on the Civil War are easily classified. The biographies of
Lee and Jackson together cover the main events of the war
in Virginia. *Surry of Eagle's-Nest* is a close parallel of
Jackson, just as *Mohun* is of *Lee*—the major events are
the same, the novels having an interweaving of fiction. The
same material served further as the basis for Cooke's numerous periodical articles, the best of which he collected into
volume form under the titles *Wearing of the Gray* and
Hammer and Rapier. *Hilt to Hilt* stands slightly apart
from Cooke's other books on the War; it is a novel dealing
with Mosby's field of action, in particular the lower Valley
of Virginia.

Cooke did not find it hard to resume writing. His home
surroundings were propitious. Even while campaigning, he
had given himself considerable practice by his contributions to the Confederate newspapers, and now after the war
he frequently received letters urging him to use his pen in
defence of the prostrate South. Fitzhugh Lee even suggested the facetious title "Southern Generals, who they
are and what they done," and upon another occasion wrote:
"I send you a document—and now you, d—— it, put me on
the highest pinnacle of history that my young ones (after
I get them) may crawl up and read of their daddy's doings
in bygone days." Cooke, moreover, was always a facile
writer. His only problem now was to be more gentle in
the epithets applied to the North, and this perhaps was
not a very hard task. By the summer of 1865 he had begun
his contributions to the New York *World.* He received ten
dollars a column and the cash in hand was a godsend. The
first book he thought of was a revised biography of Jackson.

A *Life of Stonewall Jackson* had been written by Cooke
at the "persevering requests of Ayres and Wade," was published by them in Richmond in 1863, and was pirated and

brought out in New York at approximately the same time by Charles B. Richardson. This work was the basis of the bulkier *Stonewall Jackson: a Military Biography* which D. Appleton and Company published in 1866. The first book was begun ''under a breadth of canvass'' at Stuart's camp east of Orange Court House early in May, 1863, and thereafter was continued from place to place as war duties permitted. Its composition was attended by the physical difficulties occasioned by chattering officers, flaring candles, and intermittent fighting. It was ''written in a tent, on the outpost; the enemy yonder, almost in view—but with Jackson, alas! no longer in front. The real historian of his life will write in a quiet study, in the tranquil days of peace, with no enemy, let us hope, anywhere in view, on all the vast horizon of the Confederate States.'' Cooke stated that the account was given largely ''in the words of General Jackson's official reports,'' but he relied considerably upon newspaper accounts both Northern and Southern, as well as upon the testimony of eye-witnesses, including himself. The manuscript was ''entrusted to Col. Tyler A. A. G., for transmission to Richmond. But it didn't go! It was put by someone in the P. O. at Winchester, without stamps—a friend recognized my hand and paid them—and the ms, at last, about August, reached the publishers.''

With only four pages devoted to the first thirty-seven years of the life of a man who was killed at thirty-nine, the book as a life is absurdly disproportioned. It is, however, much more interesting than its expanded later edition. It is unique among Cooke's works in that it was written not in the United States, but in the Confederacy before the Southern star had begun to decline at Gettysburg. The Northern army is shown as Cooke saw it in the early summer of 1863. For many of the Federal generals he has no adverse comment, but he cannot tolerate Pope. ''Let us not speak of him with indignation, or in terms of labored insult. Opprobrious epithets cannot reach him; and the present writer would derive no satisfaction from dwelling on the fact that Gen. Pope, as all now concede, was a braggart, a poltroon, guilty of systematic falsehood; and proved to have perpetrated in his own person outrages which mark the low-born, and low-bred wretch.'' ''Booty and beauty'' is stated by Cooke to have been the watchword of Pope's army. ''Some companies seemed to be of a decent agricultural or mechanical complexion,'' he quotes from the Reverend Mr. George of Culpeper County. The Irish were not too bad, but Sigel's ''Germans'' were ''about as cleanly and intellectual as the overgrown sows of 'der Vaterland.' '' ''Next came the selected assassins and thieves, who were probably received upon certificates of their actual conviction and service in the penitentiaries. And last, and worst of all, the Puritans and psalm-singers of pious New England.'' The book is permeated with an absolute belief that Almighty God would assure the ultimate triumph of the Southern cause. Such confidence tended to lead to a last-ditch resistance and must have added a quintessence of pain to the physical calamity of defeat.

The *Life of Stonewall Jackson* is studded with superlatives and has a rapid militant style. Written under strong emotional pressure, it contains many passages which exhibit the sumptuousness of the older type of Southern public speech. With the view of having the work published in London, Cooke revised and enlarged it in the winter of 1863-64; and sent a copy, through ''Mr. Benjamin's State Department,'' to England. Commissioner Mason, to whom it was directed, wrote in the fall of 1865 that it had never been received. The original of the expanded *Jackson* was put in the hands of Cooke's sister Mary, who buried it in the earth when Richmond was burned. This copy was not lost; but was, of course, not well adapted to publication in the United States after the war. Cooke, therefore, "watered" it to suit the changed times and—despite the two wholly distinct editions—the life of Jackson as he liked it best was never given to the public.

The Appletons prepared a superb make-up for the post-bellum *Stonewall Jackson,* embellishing it with full-page engravings of the famous generals of the opposing armies, and binding some of the copies handsomely in leather decorated with gold. Meanwhile Richardson, hearing of the new book, hastened to bring out a reprint of his edition. Cooke prevented the use of his name, acknowledging the authorship for the first time, the work having previously been spoken of in the North as presumably by the Richmond editor, John M. Daniel. Richardson's reprint was followed shortly by the Appleton *Jackson,* which, according to Cooke, "was exquisitely printed, but too high priced, and had only a sale *d'estime."* Although nearly twice as long as the earlier book, the newer requires no particular comment. Like its predecessor, it is a record of campaigns in which Jackson participated, but in general deals with him not much more intimately than with other officers of high rank. It is emphatically not a biography in the usual sense. A realization of the truth of this may have influenced the substitution of "military biography" for "life" in the title of the enlarged work.

The pay from the *World* and the prospects from *Jackson* were encouraging. "I wanted ready money however," Cooke later recorded in his literary notes, "and wrote to Richardson—before our misunderstanding—saying that I 'wanted' $200: and if he would advance that amt. I would furnish him in the fall of that year with the ms. of an historical romance, bringing in Stuart etc.—a book on the war. He replied courteously that he only published *histories* but had some friends in the same building with him, to whom he would hand my letter—which he did. They were Bunce & Huntington,—Bunce being the head man,—and Bunce wrote me at once a very cordial letter, accepting my proposition and authorizing me to draw on him for $200. I did so, and remember what a fortune I considered it. I was penniless, had to borrow the paper upon which to write the *World* sketches.'' The book whose future was thus mortgaged was *Surry of Eagle's-Nest; or the Memoirs of a Staff-Officer serving in Virginia, Edited from the mss. of Colonel Surry.* Cooke intended to make the book largely autobiographical. "Occurred to me, I think this spring of 1865," he wrote, "tho' the idea had 'come across' me, I believe, in 1864 at Petersburg." Work was begun in August, but was "resumed in earnest" about September 15, the first part being almost wholly rewritten. The book was finished on November 1. The author had been frequently cheered along in the composition by visits to the Page seat of "Saratoga," and he spent a delightful Christmas at "The Vineyard"—he had on hand proof-sheets of both *Surry* and *Jackson,* and among the guests was a most attractive lady, Miss Mary Francis Page, who was later to become Mrs. Cooke.

Surry of Eagle's-Nest, to a degree unapproached by even the most subjective of the ante-bellum romances, was written out of the fullness of its author's life and experience. May Beverley, the heroine, may be taken as a portrait of Miss Page. Like the girl of the Valley, the girl of the book sings the well-known Verdi airs to an appreciative lover. Charles Beverley is perhaps Mary Page's brother Powel, who was a close friend of Cooke. Surry, like the author, is a staff-officer. General Turner Ashby's objection to searching the belongings of ladies may well have been

copied from Cooke's own recorded experience. The letter
from "N'importe" about Pelham was actually received
by Cooke. The preponderating war element was drawn
from the author's own service and observation.

The story begins in the exciting preparatory days of
Richmond in 1861. The hero, Surry, comes into contact
with a cowardly dandy, Baskerville, in company with whom
is a young woman endowed with all the beauties and virtues.
He also sees a mysterious duel in Hollywood Cemetery.
Soon, however, Surry is commissioned a captain, is assigned as aide-de-camp to Jackson, and sets out for Harper's
Ferry. Passing through the Spottsylvania wilderness he
comes upon a house inhabited by an insane woman, a
beautiful girl, and a third female, a keen-eyed treacherous-
looking employee. Nearer the Blue Ridge he is stunned
by a limb blown from a tree in a storm, and is carried to
"The Oaks," the seat of Colonel Beverley, the father of the
beauty he saw with Baskerville. May's father had covenanted
with the now dead Baskerville, Senior, that their children
should marry, and May has at fifteen engaged herself to a
now despised but persistent suitor. Surry is wholly enam-
ored of May, but as a brave man and a soldier he merely
takes a Browningesque "last ride" with her and goes away.
While in the neighborhood, however, he becomes acquainted
with the moody and retiring Mordaunt, who is always accompanied by a faithful Arab youth, Achmed. The war now
sets to work on these characters and the plot is evolved.
Baskerville, a slacker in war, is quite willing to release
May when the loss of her slaves deprives her of her wealth,
and Surry's path is made smooth. Charley marries Surry's sister, and Will Surry, the Unionist member of the
family, marries a Miss Jennie Clayton provided for the
purpose.

There remains a sub-plot—the dark and sinister element in the book. The duelists whom Surry saw in Hollywood are Mordaunt and Fenwick. The former later operates with the Confederate army; the latter, with the Federal. Some years previously Mordaunt was successful in winning the affections of a girl whom the two men loved. Fenwick, nursing a desire for vengeance, thereupon caused the wife to leave home with him by pretending through a forged letter that the temporarily absent husband requested it. A victim of "puerperal fever" she lost her mind and was confined in an asylum, Mordaunt being informed that she had eloped with the evasive Fenwick. In the rough and tumble times of the war, Mrs. Mordaunt's innocence is established and she dies, whereupon Mordaunt marries Violet Grafton, who is a living physical duplicate of the dead woman in her youthful courtship days. After many combats Fenwick is killed, not by Mordaunt but by the latter's faithful Achmed who receives his own death-wound, his exit being necessary, since he and his master love the same woman. In the general disentanglement of the plot, Mordaunt finds the son whom he has never seen. For this young man, who has been known as Harry Saltoun, a Miss Henrietta Fitzhugh is provided as a wife.

"Has the reader forgotten Miss Henrietta Fitzhugh?" asks the author who rightly supposes the characters difficult to keep up with, since many of them appear only occasionally in the lulls between the battles. In one place, more than a hundred pages deal uninterruptedly with the war. "It appears to me that my memoirs are becoming a pure and simple history of the war in Virginia," writes Surry. The alternate consideration of great events and the fates of the characters is common to historical novelists, but in the present case the actual persons are delineated with as great minuteness as the fictitious ones, and no distinction is made between them. *Surry* is at once a reflection of its author's faults and an earnest of what he might have achieved. If Cooke had forgotten his over-worked Irvingesque habit of "editing" a supposed manu-script, had left out the Mordaunt-Fenwick plot, had even left out the big events of history, and—as he first intended —had given in his fluent, agreeable style an account of his experiences, his book might have been of perennial interest. In its actual form *Surry* has too much history to be ex-cellent fiction; and it mingles the real Farley, Pelham, and others with fictitious persons of the same and higher rank to such a degree that as history it is sometimes confusing and in small details actually misinforming. The attempted blending of two distinct elements, a wildly improbable Gothic tale and a record of a career in the Civil War, re-sults in a species of romance for which no large numbers of later general readers—boys perhaps excepted—are likely to have a pronounced taste.

The composition of *Surry* occupied about six weeks, and the results of the haste are plainly seen. Portions of *Stone-wall Jackson* are incorporated bodily. There are stylistic faults. Rapidity of composition may be blamed for such banalities as a "long farewell to the only woman he had ever loved," but it is hard to believe that so practiced a writer as Cooke would have introduced the chapters "Ar-cades Ambo" and "Mordaunt's Secret," in which Fenwick —solely for the benefit of Surry, who is at the window-shutter and must be informed somehow—narrates Mor-daunt's history to the Parkins woman who knows it already. Cooke furthermore almost revives the dead. Fenwick is once referred to as "dying." Several years later he is pinned to a tree by a sword-thrust through the middle and is left drooping and seemingly dead. The illustrator of the book gave him a most thoroughly dooming wound, as he should have done in following the text, but again the villain comes back alive. Each of these reappearances is a distinct shock to the reader. The Arabic-speaking Mordaunt and his Arab servant prove that, after all, the war was not in itself sufficiently romantic for Cooke, who sought in the Old World the most melodramatic part of his plot. *Surry* owes something to *Henry St. John*. The Mordaunt-Fenwick and Ralph-Foy pairs are similar. Parkins is of the breed of Miss Carne. The gloomy world-traveled Mordaunt inevitably suggests Byron and the titular hero of Mrs. Augusta Evans Wilson's *St. Elmo*. The behavior of the insane wife may well have been suggested by *Great Expectations* as hostile critics were not averse to pointing out. George Cary Eggleston, taking up Bagby's criticism, already referred to, said of *Surry* that its author indeed *"had the pink goggles,"* but that they were important now to give the sanity and the perspective of history to recent events. In doing this he felt Cooke to be without parallel. Whether or not this praise is too high, *Surry* was above all else a timely book. It was not penned with the care expected in a great modern historical novel. It must, however, have afforded pleasant reading to many a veteran; for it showed the war not as a failure, but as a superb adventure, the very participation in which was a mark of honor. Even to-day it is an agreeable volume for Southerners and others who are interested in the Civil War, like a stirring tale, and do not read too critically. Upon its appearance *Surry* had an excellent sale. It was published in February, 1866, and by the end of 1870 Cooke had received from it over $2,313. Smaller royalties continued. Financially this was the most successful of his novels. The interest in war stories waned with great rapidity, and no one of Cooke's later romances secured so definite a hold on popular approval.

Cooke went to New York in the early spring of 1866.

"Saw Gen. Cooke," he writes, "and was received with the warmest affection by him and Aunt as I expected. I always felt as if I had much more against him than he against me. . . . Duyckinck was a good friend and as kind as ever, going with me everywhere. Was at Appleton's, Huntington's, Scribner's, etc., and everywhere courteously received—old W. H. Appleton assuring me he was greatly pleased to see me. . . . Scribner proposed *Wearing of the Gray*—the sort of book: not the title, which he wished afterwards changed to *Lee and His Lieutenants* (a title proposed to him by myself, abandoned by me as unsuitable for the book; and then Mr. Pollard adopted the name, publishing with Treat & Co., of which firm Scribner was a member)." In view of this account of his reception in the North it is somewhat surprising that Cooke should say of the same trip: "I can't bear the Yankees: like them less than ever. They and we are two people." It should be remembered, however, that Cooke was writing in 1866.

About this time Cooke was offered by Richardson $2000 for a work on the "heroic women of the South." The idea was abandoned, however, for no interesting material could be assembled. The truth was that the women's work, however noble and valuable, was not spectacular; and no vitally interesting portraits could be drawn— especially by a writer of Cooke's type of talent. Worry over the impracticable "Southern Women" and a contemplated life of Lee, "with some other private affairs which took up much time," caused the compilation, *Wearing of the Gray,* to consume the summer and autumn of 1866.

Wearing of the Gray was brought out at New York in 1867 by E. B. Treat and Company. It was handsomely printed and was illustrated with "portraits engraved on steel from photographs taken from life" and with "battle scenes from original designs." The new volume "was made up largely of the *World, News,* and other articles, written in 1865-66, others from the Richmond Ill. News, etc., etc.," but several of the pieces—including "To Gettysburg and Back Again," "A Dash at Aldie," and "General Pegram on the Night Before His Death"—had not been previously published. *Wearing of the Gray* bears the inscription: "To the illustrious memory of Major-General J. E. B. Stuart, 'Flower of Cavaliers,' This Book is Dedicated by an old member of his Staff, who loved him living, and mourns him dead." The forty-seven component papers were classified under five heads: "Personal Portraits," "In the Cavalry," "Outlines from the Outpost," "Scout Life," and "Latter Days." A picture of Stuart was chosen as the frontispiece and a sketch of him opens the list of personal portraits. Cooke aimed "to draw these 'worthies' rather as they lived and moved, following their various idiosyncrasies, than as they performed their official duties on the public stage. . . . No personage is spoken of with whom the writer was not more or less acquainted: and every trait and incident set down was either observed by himself or obtained from good authority. Invention has absolutely nothing to do with the sketches: the writer has recorded his recollections, and not his fancies." As a staff-officer Cooke had a superb opportunity for observing the important Confederate figures in Virginia and these portraits are on the whole an entertaining and valuable piece of work. A reader of "Stuart" feels that he knows that officer, his love of music, color, and pretty women, his abhorrence of profanity and drinking, his thorough imperturbability, and his joy in the face of danger. One joins Cooke in his admiration of the great cavalryman who accomplished tasks which none of his fellows could compass, and yet refrained from repressing his individuality, amusing himself with banjo and song whether the more puritanical of his associates frowned on it or not. "Jackson" is a good short portrait condensed from the *Military Biography*. The paper on Ashby, praising a fine horseman whose example lived as an inspiration after his death, exhibits well one of the author's chief faults: even in a twelve-page sketch several details are stated more than once. Cooke recounts many interesting anecdotes about the leaders and quotes their words. The "bold, straightforward, masculine, and incisive" Early is recorded as saying to his surgeon on Lee's surrender: "Doctor, I wish there was powder enough in the center of the earth to blow it to atoms. I would apply the torch with the greatest pleasure."

Of all his army service Cooke liked best the days when he "followed the feather" of Stuart; and that favorite general figures largely in the cavalry sketches. "To the cavalryman belongs the fresh life of the forest—the wandering existence which brings back the days of old romance. Do you wish to form some conception of the life of that model cavalryman and gentleman, Don Quixote? To do so, you have only to 'join the cavalry.' Like the Don, your cavalryman goes through the land in search of adventures, and finds many. He penetrates retired localities—odd, unknown nooks—meeting with curious characters and out-of-the-way experiences, which would make the fortune of a romance writer. Here, far away from the rushing world and the clash of arms, he finds bright faces, and is welcomed by 'heaven's last best gift'—for woman is ever the guardian angel of the soldier. She smiles upon him when he is gloomy; feeds him when he is hungry; and it is often the musical laughter of a girl which the cavalryman hears as he rides on musing—not the rattle of his miserable sabre! Thus romance, sentiment, and poetry meet him everywhere. And is he fond of the grotesque? That meets him, too, in a thousand places. Of the pathetic? Ah! that salutes him often on the fierce arena of war! Thus, living a fresh life, full of vivid emotions, he passes his days and nights till the fatal bullet comes—laughing, fighting, feasting, starving, to the end.'' Cooke tells, for instance, of a raid on a deserted grocery store which caused Stuart to be acclaimed by a previously grumbling army as first of the world's soldiers; he tells of a lady who spent months in a Federal prison because there was found in her possession a joking document signed by Stuart making her an honorary staff officer. With such material the author was an adept.

Uneven as it is in quality, *Wearing of the Gray* is nevertheless both interesting and of solid value. Cooke felt that he was not only entertaining the reader of his day, but was recording for the future. In ''One of Stuart's Escapes,'' he says, ''Ah! those 'romances of the war'! The trifling species will come first. . . . But then will come the better order of things, when writers like Walter Scott will conscientiously collect the real facts, and make some new 'Waverley' or 'Legend of Montrose'.'' ''For these, and not for the former class,'' Cooke says he is setting down his incidents. A pleasing touch is given by the author's frequently addressing the unknown persons who crossed his path in the war: ''If the fair girl living in the handsome mansion below Mr. Hamilton's, remembers still to whom she insisted upon presenting nine cups of coffee with every delicacy, the rebel in question begs to assure her of his continued gratitude for her kindness.'' Unfortunately some of the papers are fiction and not history. ''Longbow's Horse,'' for instance, concludes with a reference to Colonel Surry and May Beverley, characters in *Surry of Eagle's-Nest*. The inclusion of already published articles causes several anecdotes to be repeated, as in the overlapping ''Mosby'' and ''Mosby's Raid into Fairfax.'' The separate origin of the articles results also in a style of unusual redundancy. Murat, Rupert, and other favorites are alluded to again and again in Cooke's comparisons. A small but unnecessary flaw is the use of "natale solum," "gaudium certaminis," "immedicabile vulnus," and "perdu," where English words are available. Cooke was very fond of this show of learning and kept it up despite the disapproval of critics and the constant typographical errors of his unilingual printers. His camp chimney fell flat to the ground, whereupon he began it again, "ab ovo." The "ab ovo" was printed as "above," the type-setter and many readers doubtless wondering what manner of rock-layer Cooke was.

Following the completion of *Wearing of the Gray*, Cooke began work on a somewhat similarly organized collection of twelve compositions which appeared in *The Old Guard* as *The Battles of Virginia*, an appropriate title inasmuch as Chapter I deals with First Manassas and Chapter XII with Lee's retreat and surrender. This manuscript was finished April 19, 1867; the last chapter appeared in the magazine in February, 1868; but the work was not published as a volume until 1870, when Carleton printed it as *Hammer and Rapier*, a title suggested by a figure in the "Wilderness" chapter. Cooke says of Grant's assuming command of the Federal army: "The rapier had been tried for three long years, and Lee, that great swordsman, had parried every lunge. What was his Federal adversary of the huge bulk and muscle to do now, in these last days? One course alone was left him—to take the sledge-hammer in both hands, and, leaving tricks of fence aside, advance straightforward, and smash the rapier in pieces, blow by blow, shattering the arm that wielded it, to the shoulder blade." "Honour to obstinate resolve, and the heart that does not despair. Grant had them," says Cooke of the plan of a continuous aggressive; and with regard to Grant's conduct at Appomattox he continues: "The Federal Commander had acted throughout all with the generosity of a soldier and the breeding of a gentleman.'' Cooke was honest in this recognition of merit in an opponent. Even during the war he was never bitter against McClellan, Meade, or Grant, just as in peace he still upon every occasion assailed the brutality of Sheridan and Pope. Much of Cooke's military service was in the cavalry, and in this branch the superiority of the hard-riding Southerners for the first two years was unquestioned even in the North. That he was anxious to award honor wherever due is evidenced, however, by a description of the Northern stand at Port Republic: ''Three times the Federal artillery was thus lost and won, in spite of the most desperate fighting. All honor to courage wherever it displays itself, under the blue coat or under the gray; and the Federal forces fought that day with a gallantry that was superb. They died where they stood, like brave men and true soldiers—an enemy records that and salutes them.''

Hammer and Rapier shows a certain knowledge of military tactics. The author points out that if Virginia should again be invaded from the north there would probably be new battles of Manassas, the Wilderness, and Cold Harbor. The twelve sketches largely parallel Cooke's military biographies of Jackson and Lee, and the historical portions of *Surry* and *Mohun*. For the battles, however, *Hammer and Rapier* has the superiority of being stripped of fictitious and superfluous details. The following account of Pickett's charge is far more effective than the similar but more wordy record in *Mohun:*

"The Virginians of Pickett form in double line, just in the edge of the wood on Seminary Ridge—then they are seen to move. They advance into the valley, supported by Pettigrew on the left, and Wilcox ready to follow on the right. So the division goes into that Valley of Death, advancing in face of the enemy's guns at "common time," as the troops of Ney moved under the Russian artillery, on the banks of the Dnieper.

"The two armies look on, holding their breath. It is a magnificent spectacle. Old soldiers, hardened in the fire of battle, flush and lean forward with fiery eyes. Suddenly the Federal artillery opens all its thunders, and the ranks are swept from end to end by round shot, shell, and canister. Bloody gaps are seen, but the men close up; the line advances slowly, as before. The fire redoubles; all the demons of hell seem howling, roaring, yelling, screaming, gibbering in one great witch's sabbat. Through the attacking column tears a storm of iron, before which men fall in heaps, mangled, bleeding, their bodies torn to pieces, their dying hands clutching the grass. The survivors close up the ranks and go on steadily.

"Virginia is not poor and bare, as some suppose her. She is rich beyond royal or imperial dreams—for she has that charge.

"At three hundred yards from the slope, the real conflict bursts forth. There the thunder of artillery is succeeded by the crash of musketry. From behind their stone breastwork the Federal infantry rise and pour a sudden and staggering fire into the assailants. Before that fire the troops of Pettigrew melt away. It sweeps them as dry leaves are swept by the wind. Where a moment before was a line of infantry, is now a mass of fugitives, flying wildly before the hurricane—the brave Pettigrew falling as he waves his sword and attempts to rally them.

"The Virginians have lost the flower of their forces, but the survivors continue to advance. In face of the concentrated fire of the infantry forming the Federal centre, they ascend the slope, rush headlong at the breastworks; storm them; strike their bayonets into the flying Federals; and a wild cheer rises, making the blood leap in the veins of a hundred thousand men.

"They are torn to pieces, but they have carried the works. Alas! it is only the first line. Beyond, other earthworks frown; in their faces are thrust the muzzles of muskets which spout flame—the new line, too, must be carried, and they dash at it.

"Then is seen a spectacle which will long be remembered—Pickett's little remnant charging the whole Federal army. They charge, and are nearly annihilated. Every step death meets them. Then the enemy close in on the flanks of the little band—no supporters are near—they fight bayonet to bayonet, and die.

"When the torn and bleeding remnant fall back from the fatal hill, pursued by yells, shouts, musket balls, cannon shot, they present a spectacle which would be piteous if it were not sublime. Of the three brigades, a few scattered battalions only return. Where are the commanders? The brave Garnett killed; the gallant Armistead mortally wounded as he leaped his horse over the breastworks; the fiery Kemper lying maimed for life, under the canister whirling over him. Fourteen field officers out of fifteen are stretched dead and dying on the field. Of the men, three-fourths are dead or prisoners. "The battle of Gettysburg is decided."

The day he finished *Hammer and Rapier* Cooke "got the sequel to *Surry* on the brain." "I however rec'd a proposition from Slater & Co., of the Balt. 'Home Journal' to write a story for them, and agreed to do so. . . . This led to the writing of *Monksden, or the Fate of the Calverts,* which was commenced in June, 1867 (before the 9th), and finished July 25, 1867. Written in 27 working days exactly. Revised in 2." The story was founded on the old "Tragedy of Hairston," which had appeared in *Putnam's Monthly* in 1856, and was composed with facility. Cooke sold it to Slater for $1300, reserving the right to print it as a book after five years. The magazine rights were later disposed of by the *Home Journal* to the Philadelphia *Saturday Night,* but *Monksden* never appeared as a volume.

Still another work intervened between *Hammer and Rapier* and the "sequel to *Surry*." Before the completion of *Monksden,* Cooke had been asked by W. J. McClellan to write a novelette for his *Southern Society,* another Baltimore periodical. Though somewhat fatigued from the work on *Monksden,* he wrote *Hilt to Hilt* between August 8 and September 11, 1867. This he thought was very slow composition. "Jaded by work, however, and the hot weather, I could not go to it *con amore.*" For the manuscript Cooke asked and received $500. Carleton wished to buy the story from Cooke, but the Baltimore editor naturally refused permission, and sold it himself to Carleton, who paid Cooke for revising and enlarging it.

Hilt to Hilt appeared as a book in 1869. The scene is laid on the banks of the Shenandoah River between Winchester and the Blue Ridge. This territory was part of "Mosby's Confederacy," a name applied to the portion of Virginia north of the Rappahannock and along the lower Shenandoah, a region which throughout the war was a no-man's-land. The fictitious Surry is on a "tour of duty" from Lee's army to Early's and takes part in the incidents which he works up in 1868 into an "episodical memoir." The book lacks the large figures of history, the battles, the sweep, but it has essentially the plot of *Surry*. The two Arden brothers are fighting on opposite sides. Ellen Adair is, by the machinations of the jealous villain, Ratcliffe, estranged from her lover, Landon. The strain of foreign blood, Basque this time, is found in Antoinette Duvarnay. The villains are at length overcome and a happy outcome is provided for such of the virtuous as are not gloriously dead. *Hilt to Hilt* is notable in that it deals with Cooke's home community. Annie Meadows is courted and won by the Confederate Arden at "The Briars," later Cooke's home. "Pagebrook," the seat of the father of his future wife, is called by name. The village of Millwood and the town of Winchester are apostrophized. In his prologue Cooke incorporates some adverse Boston criticism. "I had supposed the ms. of *Surry of Eagle's-Nest* to have been composed in a most compact, terse, and altogether faultless style; and here was a great critic, and a critic in Boston, which was worse still, declaring that I was florid and exaggerated! What to do? . . . I could only resolve that, in future, I would never be florid or exaggerated any more." He asserts the substantial truthfulness to actuality of the incidents in *Hilt to Hilt*, remarks that from fear of being called

a "sensation-writer" he leaves out some of the more exciting details; states, in fine, that he is aiming to "tell a plain
and unadorned story." It is nevertheless difficult to see
how he can have been serious in this pretension, for in
incident and in style *Hilt to Hilt* is as melodramatic as can
well be imagined. What else could be said of this selection?

" 'Let me finish. For the last three days his infatuation has
become a species of madness. He has repulsed, insulted, spurned,
put his heel upon me! I am no longer anything but the wretched
slave of his caprice! He has made nothing of telling me that I
am disgusting in his eyes. He has dared to use a term in addressing
me that I will not repeat! Yes, this man, to whom I have sacri-
ficed everything,—for whom I have lost name and fame, and all
that a woman values,—this base, cowardly wretch, who has lied and
tricked and betrayed others for so long, has now insulted, outraged,
and betrayed me.

" 'He has betrayed me,' continued the speaker with flaming eyes;
'but woe to him! He has not counted on the Basque blood of the
Duvarnays! I have but one aim,—to crush him! And now, perhaps, you understand why I have come hither, Captain Landon.
I come to say, you have only to follow me to surprise and destroy
the bitterest enemy you have in the world! I will lead you straight
to him; will deliver him into your hands, asking one thing only—
that you will allow me to be present when you bury your sword in
his cowardly heart!' "

Mohun; or The Last Days of Lee and His Paladins, the
sequel to *Surry of Eagle's-Nest*, was begun in January and
was finished about the middle of April, 1868. "It took
three months of solid work," said the author. "I worked
harder on this than on any book I have ever written; and
I think it more compact, and durable." *Mohun* was accepted by F. J. Huntington and was published promptly.
It requires no detailed comment for its merits and defects are those of *Surry*. Personal anecdotes, history, and
terroristic fiction are again offered in combination. The
titular hero is a Confederate general who believes himself to

be a married man and a murderer, but finds at the appointed time that he is neither. The beautiful evil woman, the hidden identity, the love of the same woman, and other of Cooke's relished characters and devices are here repeated. The leading villain is known first as Darke, then as Mortimer, and finally as Davenant. Some expert spies, an attempted poisoning, a negro sorceress, numerous melodramatic adventures—all these are made use of and the expected quota of love affairs is not omitted. Some of the characters of *Surry* reappear. The plot further involves ante-bellum trials and family altercations, and is very complex—to outline it here is unnecessary. The greatest value of the work lies in its depiction of the dogged determination of the lessening band of "Lee's Miserables"[1] as they faced defeat, and in the admirable representation of the civilian classes in Richmond: the colonel awaiting a brigadiership before beginning to fight, the food speculators and others laying the financial foundations for a newer degraded aristocracy while the finest sons of the Old Dominion were sacrificing their lives as well as their wealth. It was a pity to waste the seed-corn of the race, thought Cooke and the best Virginians, but why should it be saved if there would be no sacred Southern soil where it might flourish? The style of the book is facile and not uniform in texture. It sometimes has a tinge of the yellow-back; but in places, as in the invocation to the field of Gettysburg, exhibits an ornate splendor. To one who reads Cooke's works in their chronological order, a large portion of the military matter is now familiar, and the lack of variety in expression begins to pall. Again and again are found such phrases as "hilt to hilt" and "hammer and rapier," to cite

---

[1] Many of Lee's men applied to themselves the humorously mispronounced title of Victor Hugo's *Les Misérables*, a novel which, according to Cooke, was very popular among the Confederate soldiers.

only those figures which give names to books. Once or twice Cooke forgot his rôle of historian and spoke out in the present. He meant it from his heart when he inserted an appeal to the states carved from the territory ceded by Virginia to the federal government: "In February, 1868, when these lines are written, black hands have got Virginia by the throat, and she is suffocating—Messieurs of the great Northwest, she gave you being, and suckled you! Are you going to see her strangled before your very eyes?"

As early as 1866 Cooke had given thought to writing a life of Robert E. Lee. A letter to the general elicited a reply which he did not consider enthusiastic, so he abandoned the project. Lee's letter, however, as Cooke later concluded, indicated no more objection than would have been voiced by any modest man. At all events, immediately upon the death of the great soldier on October 12, 1870, D. Appleton and Company offered Cooke $1500 for a biography, and he accepted the commission. Before the end of October he had begun to write, and finished his task in forty-five working days. He mailed the last of the manuscript on January 19, 1871, the significance of the date as Lee's birthday apparently not occurring to him, for he did not record it in his diary.

The *Life of General Robert E. Lee* is, in its portraits, illustrations, and maps, and its type and binding, a fitting companion to the *Stonewall Jackson*. In method and style the two biographies are so nearly identical that the second calls for no extended comment. It is a narrative of Lee's campaigns in Virginia, Maryland, and Pennsylvania— almost no attention whatever is paid to the years before 1861 or after 1865. For battles and other national events one can have recourse to a history; a biography should reveal at least a few personal idiosyncrasies. There is always great curiosity over the youth and the old age of a genius

or a hero, and Lee was both. In Cooke's *Life* the great general is, at the close of five hundred pages, still but a distant
figure passing on horseback. The military leader may have
been revealed; the man is largely unknown. In such matters
as he does admit, Cooke distributes emphasis rather poorly.
Lee's four years at West Point are dismissed in a line, while
a chapter is devoted to his visit to the death-bed of the
Episcopalian bishop, William Meade. It must be borne in
mind, however, that Cooke produced this book rapidly to
meet a sudden popular demand, and made use of only such
facts as he knew or could discover easily. He thoroughly
realized the limitations of the work. For instance, he did
not dwell upon General Lee's presidency of Washington
College, but deliberately left the subject "to a more important authority."

On his experiences in the Civil War, Cooke based seven
books, of which *Lee* was the last. In producing these works
his immediate surroundings were happy, but his outlook
was depressing. He saw his beloved Virginia in the toils of
a mismanaged reconstruction, the prey of the blacks; and
he thought he detected an approaching schism between the
different classes of whites. He refers frequently to writing
his fiction as a relief from the world about him—a circum-
stance which may account in part for his search for the
bizarre. The true tragedy of this period of his life was,
however, neither the fall of the Confederacy nor the humil-
iation attendant upon Reconstruction. It seems almost a
loss to the world that the young captain of artillery, an
already famous novelist, should have written his biographies without regard to style or sufficient data, and above
all should have vitiated notes of the utmost value by blending with them an outworn strain of fiction. What an
opportunity he lost! How famous he might have become
as the only writer of note who served from First Manassas

to Appomattox and set down with accuracy and brilliancy
the little as well as the large aspects of the great struggle!
Such a work—alas unwritten!—would have been a classic
for the twentieth century.

The reason for Cooke's apparent failure to make the most
of his material is suggested by a conversation in which he
outlined to Eggleston his attitude toward war:

"'I wasn't born to be a soldier,' he said . . . in after years. 'Of
course I can stand bullets and shells and all that, without flinching,
just as any man must if he has any manhood in him, and as for
hardships and starvation, why, a man who has self-control can
endure them when duty demands it, but I never liked the business
of war. Gold lace on my coat always made me feel as if I were a
child tricked out in red and yellow calico with turkey-feathers in
my headgear to add to the gorgeousness. There is nothing intellectual about fighting. It is fit work for brutes and brutish men.
And in modern war, where men are organized in masses and con-
verted into insensate machines, there is really nothing heroic or
romantic or in any way calculated to appeal to the imagination!'"

Cooke, in fine, was never at heart a soldier. He was a
humanitarian, a sentimentalist, a romancer, and a democrat. It was only natural that such a man should have
idealized his Civil War stories, even at a loss of the flavor
of reality.

CHAPTER IV

THE PROBLEMS OF RECONSTRUCTION—WRITER AND FARMER

JOHN ESTEN COOKE was married on September 18, 1867, to Miss Mary Francis Page, daughter of Dr. Robert Page of "Saratoga," Clarke County, Virginia. The ceremony was performed by the Reverend Joseph Jones in Christ (Episcopal) Church at Millwood. Cooke had known Miss Page for a number of years. In his diary kept in the fifties he had mentioned her casually as a fellow-guest at a mountain summer-resort. Moreover, in a contemporaneous newspaper account of an ante-bellum tournament he had praised her most highly. A deep or permanent interest in Miss Page cannot, however, be inferred from this slight evidence; for she had been crowned queen of love and beauty, and the tribute to her—while more glowing than that bestowed on her maids of honor—was no greater than custom demanded upon such an occasion. The possibility that Cooke may have had personal interest back of his praise of the youthful "queen," or that she admired him, is, nevertheless, suggested by a rather unusual document of about the same period. Sallie Goodrich, one of Miss Page's schoolmates, was required to write a composition in French, and chose as the subject of the neatly written yet somewhat ungrammatical paper an account of the supposed marriage of Miss Page to the young novelist, John Esten Cooke. This incident happened ten years before the Cooke-Page wedding, and cannot be regarded as of very serious import, for during the war the author-soldier was fancy-free, and after the war his love for Miss Page appears to have been altogether as new as it was deep and whole-hearted. He refers to her as the anchor which held him to Virginia when, in the disappointment of defeat, he had determined on leaving the state and nation. A glimpse of the zealous lover may be had from the article "I Go To See John Esten Cooke" which G. W. Bagby wrote and published in his *Orange Native Virginian*. Cooke's diary, indeed, reveals the fact that he frequently visited "Saratoga," and Bagby good-naturedly states that even the guest was neglected by the novelist who hurried away on horseback to keep a previous engagement with his lady.

Cooke not only married a charming woman, but he married into a family as notable as his own. Perhaps for the very reason that his social standing was unquestioned and soundly based, he was never a snob. He was a typical representative of the saner democratic element in the mid-nineteenth century aristocracy of Virginia. An illustration of his family's attitude toward snobbery may be found in Cooke's reaction to a society flurry in Richmond during the war. A volunteer committee had spent time and money in preparing to stage an elaborate tableau performance for war relief. Cooke's sister Mary, Mrs. Steger, wrote him about it: "The Misses ————, and one or two other *fashionable* young ladies, who had *promised* to take part in the performance, have declined; they gave as their excuse, they heard the ———————— were not *fashionable*." Mrs. Steger explained that the family—with whose representative the ladies of fashion would not appear on the stage —was thoroughly estimable, and begged her brother to come if possible and help save the occasion. The sum total of such unsocial acts on the part of a set of small-brained girls was, as Cooke sorrowfully knew, of indirect aid to the

Federal soldiers in precipitating the fall of the Confederacy. Such types he held in contempt and flayed them in
Mohun along with the profiteer and the colonel who was
waiting to be made a general before drawing his sword.
Just as Cooke never made ignoble use of his distinguished
birth, he never failed, on the other hand, to feel in it a
restrained pride. He was pleased that his sister Sal, Mrs.
Duval, was "regarded as the *first person in New Kent*.
Somehow we stand high wherever we go. It is singular,
isn't it?" He was fond of recalling George Cary Eggleston's "joke": "Somebody asked somebody else who [*sic*]
J. Esten Cooke married. The reply was Miss Page—a big
connection—he had married into all the good families he
didn't belong to himself."

Cooke's wedding was followed by a "tour" which extended "East and North" as far as Quebec and Niagara
Falls. Upon his return to Virginia he settled with his
bride at her father's home, where he continued his profession of writing. The stay at "Saratoga" was altogether
pleasant. The novelist relieved the routine of composition
by occasional work in the garden. He often went fishing,
and caught, he records, as many as twenty fish on one trip.
He "bathed in the run under the willow," used "Pride of
Virginia" tobacco, and would sit "under the lindens smoking" as he watched the "magnificent moon rise over the
mountains." There is no indication that even a shadow of
disagreement ever passed between him and the Pages, and
he looked forward with grief to the necessity of leaving a
home made doubly dear by the genial comradeship of his
wife's family and the memories of his own early married
days. But Cooke was a man of position, and all the habits
of society pointed to the appropriateness of his being established in a house of his own. The place selected for his
residence was a Page estate known as "The Briars."

Thither Cooke often journeyed to superintend improvements, and on September 12, 1869, he moved to "The Briars," which became his home for the rest of his life.

To John Esten Cooke and Mary Francis Page there were born three children. Before the removal from "Saratoga" an only daughter, Susan Randolph, had been born. "Yesterday morning [*i. e.,* on July 11, 1868] about six o'clock Mary's daughter was born—a fine healthy child. . . . Mary is astonishingly well and gay—it is difficult to understand that she is unwell." The diary recalls many of Susie's baby antics, the father noting, for instance, that she wept when the water touched her in the christening ceremony. Cooke likewise records the birth of Edmund Pendleton, his first son: "This morning [May 23, 1870] at a quarter before eight o'clock Mary gave birth to what Cousin Lucy Mann says is a 'fine boy.' This is written a few minutes afterwards. A lovely morning." Cooke's last child was born in 1874: "At about 3 in the morning, October 12, was born our third child, a fine boy who is to be called Robert Powel Page in full after Dr. P. and Powel. Mary and the baby are quite well."

Cooke thus, in a home of his own and surrounded by his family, began to carry forward his career as a writer under conditions which were not only dear to his heart but had long been cherished as ideal before there was any promise of their fulfilment. On the last day of the year 1848 he had written to his brother Philip: "You don't know what a happy life you lead, no work—writing tales is not work, more fun than anything else—a sweet wife, fine children and nothing to do but amuse yourself." Although Cooke directed, perhaps in the mood of a moment, that his pre-war diary be destroyed, he declared on the contrary in his new one that he was writing it for his children when they should grow up. The pages abound in such entries as the following: "God bless my dear one and my little one: I wonder if anybody will laugh at that if they poach on my diary!" The entries normally close with the letters "D. N. B.," a hurried abbreviation of "Dieu nous bénisse," the sincere prayer of the husband and father.

At "The Briars" Cooke became, for the first time in his life, a gardener and farmer. He was an adept in the seed-catalogue nomenclature of his day, strove for a large variety of vegetables for his kitchen-garden, and experienced an amateur's satisfaction in producing a certain vegetable before any of the neighbors. He gave individuality to his labors and expressed his fatherly pride by planting lettuce seed in such a way that, upon coming up, they would spell the name SUSIE. "Politics, and city and public life seem to me the merest farces. Literature and gardening are the really philosophic pursuits of life." Cooke complained that gardening even disputed with writing the command of his major interest. In an opposite mood, he went so far as to revolve in his mind the idea of selling his produce in the Baltimore and Alexandria markets; but wisely concluded that he lacked the "energy, industry and system requisite for success in any such undertaking." He was also ambitious of becoming a fruit and grape grower. By experiments on his large farm he reached conclusions about the relative efficacy of manure and artificial fertilizer as crop producers. On the whole, however, he showed a lack of adaptability to his new environment. For many years he was a victim of the mistakes common to the inexperienced manager or to those who regard farming as an unskilled calling. To persons who have seen the havoc one storm may produce, or who know something of animal diseases and animal enemies, a few sentences like the following are enough to reveal Cooke as, at best, a "book-farmer": "Putting out sheep is an excel-

lent business. It is not difficult to make 100 per cent on
the investment without chance of loss, and difficult to make
less than fifty!''

Cooke's profits from writing fortunately prevented his
farming ventures from shipwrecking him; and he was en-
abled from the start to go forward with his plans for
beautifying his house and grounds. "By care and industry, with a little time," he wrote, " 'The Briars' may be
made a neat, attractive and happy-looking home." In his
improvements the author was not only the landscape artist,
but did most of the work. He planted new shrubs and
flowers, pruned trees, kept in repair the wall around the
lawn, and with his own hands built rustic outdoor seats.

In his attractive home Cooke, hospitable by taste and
heredity, was from the start a lavish entertainer. Day
after day the names of numerous guests are recorded in
his diary. Unfortunately, he thought it part of the code of
a gentleman never to work while visitors were beneath his
roof. He often regretted their curtailment of his working
hours, but never complained. In reality he enjoyed every
minute of their stay and seemed at heart to welcome the
excuse for putting aside his pen. Still, one is suspicious of
a shade of irony when he recalls that forty-five visitors had
slept at "The Briars" during his first year there, some of
them for weeks. " 'The Briars' seems to have been effec-
tually 'warmed' since our arrival!'' But when all has been
said, Cooke was almost if not quite as much of a visitor
as an entertainer. He dined abroad often, sometimes day
after day, at "The Glen," "Pagebrook," and a dozen
other fancifully named old family seats, paid an annual
visit of several weeks to "Saratoga," and long occasional
visits to "Cassilis," "The Farm," and elsewhere. He attended numerous parties and sometimes gave one, as he
records on September 10, 1870: "Last night we had some-

thing like a regular party—about 60 in all—danced to two
fiddles in the old kitchen, and had a very handsome supper
table . . . a young party . . . an agreeable evening—
or rather night—broke up at 3 o'clock." As well as to
neighborhood guests Cooke was ambitious of extending the
hospitality of "The Briars" to contemporary writers and
publishers. Among his preserved papers are perhaps a
dozen letters thanking him for invitations, and assuring him
of acceptance should anything ever enable the writer to
visit the neighborhood. Some of these invitations went to
persons whom the hospitable Southerner knew but slightly;
yet an acceptance was not altogether unusual. George Cary
Eggleston, fellow Confederate veteran, author, and editor
of *Hearth and Home,* was a pleased guest who often wrote
of Cooke's novels or of the interesting Virginian himself.

In a brief sketch entitled "About the Briars," Eggleston
gives an entertaining account of Cooke's home. "Strangest
of all is the name of the hospitable mansion in which these
words are written. It stands on a grassy knoll in the midst
of the dream-like beauty of the Shenandoah Valley. As one
looks out from its wide-open portal, the Blue Ridge on the
one hand, the Alleghanies on the other, with the 'Three
Sisters' in front, inclose a very fairy-land of peaceful loveliness, whose people—all akin to each other, of course—
are just such delightful neighbors as one would want to live
among forever. The place itself is a fit center to the landscape, and its master and mistress are a part of the place.
The mansion, with its surrounding acres, is called 'The
Briars,' despite the peacefulness of its ways and the wonderful pleasantness of all its paths. Its name is a misnomer,
of course, and yet we would not have it changed on any
terms. The contrast between the homestead's thorny name
and the thornless character of its life is a constant delight.
Its master is a writer of books which everybody loves to

read. He has a delightful habit of seeing the better side of everything, and reflecting something of his own geniality upon all the men and things with which he comes in contact. He thinks well of the world, and when he talks or writes of its people they really seem better even than they think themselves. He is in the garden at this moment gathering tomatoes and cucumbers for dinner, and they are sure to come to the house looking the better for their passing through his hands. Briars couldn't grow under his eyes if they would. As he looked at them they would certainly shed their thorns and put forth flowers instead.'' Among numerous praises of autumn scenes Cooke found occasion to set down an approval of his home as it appeared in spring: ''Everything around 'The Briars' is now green and flourishing and beautiful—the grass plot like emerald, but starred with dandelions, the ashes putting forth their light tender green, the redbuds in full blossom, the wheat fields of deep rich green and lovely when the sun is on them —all bright and cheerful.'' So much for the physical side. The novelist's life at ''The Briars'' had, however, a somber aspect which grew partly out of his inability as a manager and partly out of a naturally slow adaptability to the new issues of life in the Reconstruction period.

Cooke, as has been hinted, experienced his share of the post-bellum gloom natural to an ex-Confederate officer. He saw a civilization in ruins and amid the ruins could see at first no quick seeds of hope which he felt might later develop along lines he would think desirable. The intellectual class in the South was especially hard hit by the result of the war. While the farmer for the most part still owned his land or portions of it, the writer—in many cases before the war already accustomed to live up to or beyond his earning power—found his familiar periodicals defunct or impoverished and his reading public generally too poor to buy books. Authors may also have well felt a certain chagrin upon realizing that the war's inevitability had been partly due to their attitude. The ante-bellum Southern writer had not yet learned that books like *Uncle Tom's Cabin*, irrespective of their accuracy, could not be treated with contempt, but demanded a forceful reasoned answer before the tribunal of an interested world. Southern men of letters had offered little or no help to the Southern publicists in solving the problems of the day. Some writers, indeed, upheld slavery, but in terms too exaggerated to excite respect. Others, like Cooke—who, if not actually opposed to slavery, was at least indifferent to its continuance—seemed to seek, consciously or unconsciously, in an idealized past a refuge from the fermenting world about them. After the war many of these writers realized keenly their mistake. Physically the South was prostrate: it was a duty to change tactics and defend her honor. The struggle of arms was over, but upon the Southern writer lay the solemn obligation of upholding before posterity the ideals of the Confederacy. Expressions of this view were numerous, and a self-dedication to this purpose was often urged upon Cooke by Beauregard, P. M. B. Young, and others. To thinking people Southern writers have justified the Southern attitude, but much of the work has been done by authors who have begun their careers since 1865. The impoverished professional writer of the old régime, as William Gilmore Simms declared in a review of one of Cooke's novels, was unfortunately not always wholly free in the late sixties to write what he wished. He had of necessity to write whatever would bring the most money quickly. Timrod's despair, Hayne's relative poverty, and Lanier's noble struggle are familiar to all students of American literature. Cooke presents a somewhat different case financially, for he produced a better-paying type of composition, was unmarried in the worst years, and furthermore acquired by marrying Miss Page a valuable farm. While he thus had no struggle with actual want, he was nevertheless in a position to see Reconstruction not only from the point of view of the Southern apologist, but from that of the actual rebuilder of the South's material prosperity—the farmer, confronted with market and labor problems.

Between the close of the war and March, 1873, Cooke had earned thirteen thousand dollars from his writings, but in spite of this income and his fertile farm, he was at the end of the latter year still in debt. The amount owed was only one hundred dollars, and of course reflected not hardship but careless spending, as the following record shows: ". . . great event of the parlour carpet. It was bought early in November [1869] with a part—$50 or so—of $300 I got from English for the *Heir of Gaymount*. The rug has swans on it [1]—coincidence; as a swan is one of the chief characters in the heir! . . . the parlour with all its red is quite cheerful . . ." How Cooke could enjoy a rug purchased at the price of remaining in debt seems a mystery to one familiar with his valiant struggle with his father's obligations in the fifties; but the debt was nominal and the record of it may have actually been prompted by a pride in financial integrity.

Fluctuating grain prices, occasioned by undeterminable or far-off causes like the Franco-Prussian War, were a source of great annoyance to the farmer-author, who chafed at the gamble whereby he might pay high prices for fertilizer and seed and encounter a calamitous fall in the price of wheat before harvesting his crop. He worried also over the numerous excessively bad crop years in the sixties and

[1] "Susie feeds them with crumbs in a way charming to behold." (Footnote to the entry in the diary.)

seventies; but the great problem was labor. Except for occasional tasks, Cooke did not rely on negro workmen. This was perhaps because of the relative scarcity of negroes in the Valley county of Clarke, for he seems never to have had a grudge against any member of that race. Both his mammy and his wife's mammy lived with him, and Sawney, sold before the war as an incorrigible, was often back now to regale the children with his amusing yarns. Cooke corresponded with an immigrant employment bureau in New York in the hope of securing a foreign farm-hand, but soon decided to rent. Rent he did to a succession of tenants, but never with satisfactory results. One was too slow, one was too delicate, one was a fair talker but a poor performer: thus went the unfortunate series. He wondered why he never got a desirable tenant, the true answer of course being that, with the decline of so many land-holding families, an industrious farm laborer or renter could with relative ease better his position and pass into the proprietor class. Cooke's early post-war gloom over Virginia's social and economic future was soon, by this very condition, changed to complacency, for he observed in 1882 that the new white landholders sympathized with the problems of the older aristocracy. This racial solidarity of the whites under the tutelage of ex-Confederate leaders rescued Virginia from Reconstruction and, as elsewhere in the South, put into power a political régime that has not yet been seriously disturbed.

For several years following the Civil War, Cooke was silently antagonistic to the Federal government. He resented his District Number One taxes. "Hurrah, we are as good as the freedmen!" he wrote of the amnesty proclamation which restored the voting right to ex-Confederate soldiers. On July 4, 1870, he wrote: "Grand humbug of 'celebrations'!—in which the South, having no independence to celebrate, takes no part! Singular how completely we rebellious ones have come to despise the United States, their flag, and all concerning them.'' In the early seventies Cooke frequently exchanged letters with the French critic, A. de Pontmartin, and compared the condition of the South with that of France. A decade, however, sufficed for the effacement of every trace of hostility. No unpleasantness resulted from his thoughts or his associations on his northern trip in 1876. On this journey he paid a two-day visit to the Centennial Exposition, spent several days in the homes of G. W. Carleton and G. C. Eggleston, and called upon O. B. Bunce, J. W. Harper, and Henry Mills Alden.

In the eight years from 1870 until the death of his wife Cooke produced a half-score of books which, in their setting and time, varied from the seventeenth century England of *Her Majesty the Queen* to the contemporary America of *Pretty Mrs. Gaston.* The novels of this decade are more nearly forgotten than those of any other period of Cooke's activity, but while they are not notable they do not deserve aggressive condemnation. They are in many cases good of their kind, and doubtless gave satisfaction to such of their readers as did not peruse them with too critical an eye.

Among these novels there is one, not the best of the lot, considered as literature, which stands out as of the highest interest. *The Heir of Gaymount* contains an almost complete record of Cooke's response to his environment in the years immediately following the war. There were in the South thousands of farmers but few professional writers. Perhaps because he belonged to each class, Cooke tried to give through literature an admonitory message to the farmer. While working on the book, he called it ''Truck.'' His ideas in regard to farming and other Reconstruction problems are fastened upon a conventional plot.

Edmund Carteret, formerly lieutenant in the Confederate States army, finds himself the heir of "Gaymount," an old family seat in Virginia on the South bank of the Potomac River. Along with the mansion-house, however, Carteret receives but forty acres of land. The late owner, an uncle of Federal sympathies, has been angered at Edmund's service to the Confederacy, and has left him only what he felt to be inherently due him as the bearer of the family name. The bulk of the property has been left to another nephew, Arthur Botleigh. Edmund not only has never worked, but he is penniless; he sits amid his decaying possessions and mopes. Shall he join Maximilian's army in Mexico, or shall he buy more land and undertake farming? In either case money is needed. Meanwhile he has remained closely at home, has not read a newspaper, and is consequently caught in a tax snare. He did not turn in by the prescribed time a list of his property, and has to accept the appraiser's assessment, which is ten times a reasonable value. To meet this tax he contemplates selling the family plate but is prevented from doing so by the opportune arrival of Frank Lance of the New York *Bird of Freedom* who pays for a horse furnished him during the war. Carteret admits to Lance that he has been contemplating writing a book. Lance advises him: "Abandon your grand ideas of writing a big volume or volumes, and write some sketches. . . . I have found out that to *do* one small thing is better than resolving only to do five hundred big things. . . . Come down to small things, above all, to *work*. Do that and you shall be great, glorious, and happy." Edmund of course has a sweetheart and an enemy in the neighborhood. The enemy is one Tugmuddle, an overseer, who ruined Carteret's father and, determined now to become owner of "Gaymount," is constantly urging Edmund to accept a loan. Major Vawter, father of Carteret's sweetheart, Annie, owes eight thousand dollars to Tug-muddle and is infuriated when the socially ambitious rascal offers to cancel the debt if Annie will marry his son. For Annie's sake Carteret gives a deed for eight thousand dollars on "Gaymount," and relieves the Vawters. He is thus rather seriously embarrassed but happens to read a torn newspaper containing an account of a gentleman who purchased forty acres of poor land in New Jersey and got rich on it by trucking. Carteret thereupon determines to raise vegetables and fruits. He enlists for his trucking crusade Rautzahn, a German gardener, and Guy Hartrigger, a member of his old company who has never left him. The events so far chronicled take place in the autumn of 1865, whereafter the curtain is lowered for three years. When it is raised Carteret is presented as having actually cleared over eight thousand dollars from his forty acres. But the money is now due to Tugmuddle, and the failure of a bank dissipates six thousand of it. Frank Lance comes on another visit. He reports that Carteret's sketches, collected as "The Greys and the Blues" have had a sale of over half a million copies. This, unfortunately, helps little, for Lance, not suspecting such success, has sold the work outright for a thousand dollars. The jolly reporter is, however, a needed visitor, for worry is hanging rather heavily over Edmund much to the grief of Annie, now his wife. The "heir" is wrought up over an effort to solve some enigmatic abbreviations found, in the handwriting of his uncle, on a piece of paper which a pet swan has pulled out from a crack in an article of furniture. Carteret finally solves the cryptogram, digs at the designated hour and place, and discovers a chest loaded with money and jewels and containing a later will of his uncle deeding him all the property. This will completely undoes Tugmuddle who has loaned over thirty thousand dollars to the now dead Botleigh. The plot is concluded with the marriage of Lance to Annie's sister, and with Hartrigger's marriage to Rose Lacy, a young Irish widow about whom he has often been good-naturedly teased by Edmund.

An outline of this commonplace plot fails to reveal the true character of *The Heir of Gaymount,* and does not explain its importance to a person interested in Cooke or in contemporary attempts at solving the problems of Reconstruction. In the first place Carteret is plainly Cooke. The author and his created hero are identical in the divided allegiance of their families, their service as Confederate company officers, their desire upon first thought to leave their humbled native state, and their marrying a young woman of the neighborhood. Carteret also writes; the sketches of "The Greys and the Blues," recall of course *Hammer and Rapier* and, in particular, *Wearing of the Gray.* The coming of the New York writer, the intense interest in gardening, and the worry over District Number One taxes are further parallels. Lance called Carteret's baby "Little Miss Rat," "Lambpig," "Mrs. Smallweed,"' and a number of other epithets which Cooke bestowed playfully on his own baby daughter.

More important even than this reflection of the author is the book's preaching of the doctrine of work as a remedy for the South's troubles. Cooke not only saw certain old families face facts and maintain their status, but he witnessed sadly the decline of others through lack of industry and initiative. His book might be taken as, in part, an appeal to the latter type of Virginian. The hero was "one of a class more numerous than the world supposes . . . the class of idlers with the capacity to perform hard work, if they can only get a clear idea of how to begin." "Begin with what you have," summarizes Cooke's admonition given in the widely quoted poem "My

Acre,'' and in the volume under consideration. " 'I have been an idler up to this time,' said the young man; 'I am going to try to become industrious, and I hope well to do. I have been living in cloudland, and I mean to come down to solid ground. I have been planning and scheming, and dreaming how I could buy land, and make money cultivating it. . . . What I mean to do now is, to give up all such fancies of adding to my estate, to cultivate what I have, and to make this tract of forty acres bring me as much as four hundred or a thousand.' '' The advice was excellent and was much needed in the South, but Cooke's application of it to the persons of the story results in a financial success so extraordinary as to be almost absurd. Making no allowances for possible loss, he almost literally counts an earned coin for each seed sown. The inadaptability of a particular crop to a particular soil and the glutting of markets have no terrors for the fortunate heir of "Gaymount." Cooke urges Virginia as a superb place for grape culture, describes the cabbage as a "noble vegetable," and even goes so far as to present a summarizing balance-sheet of the truck-farmer's transactions:

"2 acres of late cabbages, in ground from which chevril roots were taken in July:—8,400 cabbages . . . $672.00."

Thus are itemized tomatoes, peas, melons, cucumbers, horse-radish, and other vegetables.

Although the chief function of *The Heir of Gaymount* was to deliver an exhortation to the author's contemporaries, the book has certain other aspects of minor interest. It presents a quiet defence of the old Southern order. Carteret says of the pride of birth:

"The culprit before you was born in Virginia—he naturally loves it therefore, and perhaps some of its faults even. Had he a grandfather? It is probable; most people have. And he pleads guilty to possessing some old pictures, a little old silver, and even a torn family tree! Is he 'one of the wicked' for that reason? Heaven forbid! He is not responsible. These objects were here when he came; they will be here when he is gone, he hopes, and his affection for them is the result of habit, and not intended to offend anybody. Doubtless, elsewhere in the world there are many houses, with pictures and silver and family trees in them. If their owners derive innocent satisfaction from their possession, why should I think hard of it or they of me?''

Cooke, lifelong exponent of kindness, quieted and milked ''the Rose heifer'' when she would stand for no one else. Carteret says here of the wounded swan which he took home as a pet, ''Yes; but remember the swan found it. I confess I think of that often, Lance. . . . I think the fact teaches the value of kindness in this world.'' In its love-episodes the book is typical of its author. The usual contrast is afforded by the somewhat burlesquely handled affair between Guy and Mrs. Lacy, and the tender affection of the protagonists. Annie, however, is not the usual helpless heroine; she is represented as being the mainstay of the Vawter home.

Cooke devoted much thought and work to the unique *Heir of Gaymount*. Though absorbed at first by his task, he soon found the composition attended with ''unexpected difficulty.'' He had the subject in mind by January 6, 1868, began writing on August 18, but did not finish until January 25, 1869. ''Never did one small book undergo such alterations, cuttings down, remoulding, and remaking generally.'' Cooke did not readily find a publisher for his manuscript. He ''offered it to Appleton's Journal, *H. and Home*, Harpers, before English accepted it for the *Old Guard*.''

The monthly *Old Guard* and the weekly *New York Day-Book* were published by Van Evrie, Horton and Co., a publishing firm devoted to an aggressive anti-black campaign, as will be shown by some quotations from the announcements on the paper covers of *The Heir of Gaymount* which, after its appearance in the magazine, was issued as Number I of the "Old Guard Library." The *New York Day-Book* is described as being an "Independent Democratic Paper" devoted to "WHITE SUPREMACY":

"And standing now just where it did ten years ago, it therefore ignores, rejects and utterly repudiates ALL the combined efforts of fanatics, traitors and fools to MONGRELIZE the Government, and demands the RESTORATION OF THE WHITE REPUBLIC, not merely because it is best, but because the LOWER RACES cannot be incorporated in our political system without the utter destruction of Republican institutions. With a corps of writers abundantly competent to demonstrate this tremendous truth to the popular understanding, to convince the most ignorant and benighted that 'Reconstruction' is abnormal, anti-social, and forever impracticable, *The Day-Book* confidently appeals to true Democrats everywhere to come to its aid in this great cause, and save Democratic institutions from the wreck and ruin otherwise inevitable."

White Supremacy and Negro Subordination, a book by J. K. Van Evrie, was also advertised:

"It explains the suicidal policy of the Mongrel Party in trying to make races *equal* that God has made *unequal*. . . . It deals only with the fact—the fixed and everlasting fact—that God has made negroes a different and subordinate race and therefore designed them for a different and subordinate condition, and all who fail to recognize that design must, of necessity, aid in the destruction of society and the ruin of their country."

As a monograph on the problems of reconstruction *The Heir of Gaymount* belongs in the same general category with the Van Evrie-Horton publications. In contrast, however, with the tone of the above-quoted advertisements Cooke's moderation was notable, but the value of his book as a document is conspicuously lessened by his failure to consider the negro. Between diatribe and ignoring there is little to choose.

In spite of his enthusiastic effort to produce a novel economically influential and helpful, Cooke was discouraged in every way by *The Heir of Gaymount*. It was hard to write, a publisher was hard to find, and the book, when published, attracted little attention. The author was, however, writing for a livelihood, and his tales of melodramatic adventure found a ready sale. The fame of *Surry* shone in sharp contrast with the immediate oblivion of the *Heir*. It is little surprising, then, that in his next two novels he should have turned again to the past which he ever loved more than the present and, in his search for romance, should have gone as far as the rocky coast of Wales. *The Man Hunter* and *Out of the Foam* were not merely remote from what Cooke knew; they were at the opposite pole from what he had commendably undertaken in *The Heir of Gaymount*. *The Man Hunter* was begun on July 9, 1869, and finished September 6, just before Cooke moved to "The Briars." Installed in his new home he devoted the remainder of the year to the composition of *Out of the Foam,* which in manuscript was called *The Wolves of Pembrokeshire*. "I think I can make something sensational of it," wrote Cooke when he began *The Man Hunter*. "Glad it's done," he said when he finished it. He liked *Out of the Foam* "of its sort. The sort is not literature and Reade invented it to make money. I am in want thereof, and I write the *Wolves* to sell, as I would raise wheat or corn, or make coats if I were a tailor. I follow 'the fashion'—when I should set it! . . . I have attempted a style and treatment not natural to me, and I do not propose, D. V., ever again to return to it. . . . 'Out of the Foam' is mere melodrama." These two similar novels Cooke always regarded as his worst works, *The Man Hunter* appeared in the St.

Louis *Home Journal,* but was never reprinted. *Out of the Foam* "was sold, with *Fairfax,* to that jovial gentleman Mr. Carleton for $400, its full worth." It was published in 1871.

Out of the Foam deals with the adventures of Edmund Earle, a young officer of the French Navy who, during the Anglo-French struggle of the last quarter of the eighteenth century, makes a raid upon the Welsh coast. Earle visits his supposed mother, a solitary who keeps a cliff beacon burning; and, because of his nautical prowess and his knowledge of the Romany Rye, is received into membership by the "Wolves," a band of smugglers and plunderers which infests the coast. In the neighborhood lives the evil Sir Murdaugh Westbrooke who is desperately anxious to kill Earle, and drive from the country the woman who guards the beacon light. Sir Murdaugh's chiefest joy is found in the dissection of corpses, and his zealous pursuit of the strange hobby leads him to rifle the grave of a "Wolf" who has died of hydrophobia. He unwittingly infects himself from the corpse and is later seized by the malady in the presence of a crowd assembled to see him married to Elinor Maverick, a lamia of the neighborhood. In ways too complicated to outline briefly it is discovered that Earle is the long ago stolen son and heir of a popular local marquis to whom Westbrooke is the apparent next of kin; and that the old solitary is not Earle's mother but Westbrooke's wife whom he has undertaken to despatch to the West Indies before his new wedding. To the intense delight of all, from the "Wolves" to the marquis, Earle marries Elinor's cousin, the virtuous Rose Maverick.

The plot, thus briefly outlined, does not indicate fully the nature of the story. There are captures and escapes, an imprisonment in a charnel vault, sea fights, the mutilation of a marriage register, secret doors, and other incidents

and devices relished by writers of the dime-novel. Cooke
was always ashamed of *Out of the Foam*, but it is really an
excellent story of its type. It has elements of adventure,
mystery, and terror. It presents living embodiments of
physical and moral ugliness in combat with brave and
estimable persons in whose triumph one becomes something
more than quietly interested. To secure a reader's approval
a novel must be a masterly study appealing to the intellect
and reflecting true criticism of life, or, failing this, must be
either delightful or sensational. *Out of the Foam* is neither
masterly nor delightful, but it is highly sensational, and
can withal be put down unfinished less easily than some of
its author's better books.

Cooke's determination to write books of a different type
bore direct fruit. His next work in order of composition
was *Her Majesty the Queen*, a historical romance of the
downfall of Charles I. On February 10, 1870, he wrote
entirely to his "satisfaction" the first "17 pp. of the
'Story of Cecil.'" Since the new story was to be based in
part on historical fact, the author was often "greatly delayed by want of authorities of every sort." *Her Majesty
the Queen*, as the "Story of Cecil" came to be called, was
finished in thirty-two working days, but the difficulty in
securing promptly the needed source-books caused its completion to be delayed until November 16. The novel is
supposedly the memoirs of a devoted Cavalier, one Edmund
Cecil, who, when his master has been beheaded, crosses to
Virginia to establish himself on the York River. The story,
however, deals only with Edmund's adventures in England.
These are sufficiently dangerous, for ten narrow escapes
from death are chronicled. Edmund's brother Henry is
also an important figure. Each of the brothers loves Fran-
ces Villiers, and each resolves to withdraw in favor of the
other. Harry, however, soon falls in love with Alice Cary,

a niece of Lord Falkland, marries her later, and continues the English line at Cecil Court. The movements of Queen Henrietta Maria are followed rather closely, and Cooke dwells on her calmness and bravery. Although the Queen is the most prominent historical figure, attention is given to the king, Prince Rupert, the official headsman, and others; and space is devoted to the riots in London and to court life.

As a tour-de-force attempting to reproduce an atmosphere of the past, *Her Majesty the Queen* is of the manner of *Henry Esmond,* and, like *Esmond,* contains references to contemporary notables in politics and literature. Evelyn, Waller, Hampden and Milton are among those mentioned. The work aimed to afford a panorama of its period, but unfortunately lacks the little details indicative of a first-hand knowledge of the ground. The style is fluent and the incidents are well handled, but there are no high places —the narrative remains on a dead level. Cooke cherished the idea of having *Her Majesty the Queen* brought out in England, and after it was refused by the Harpers, corresponded with his friend, Colonel Peyton, who was living in Guernsey. Peyton could accomplish nothing in the way of interesting a publisher, and suggested that Cooke send the novel direct to some London firm which he might consider likely to accept it. Cooke may have remembered the loss of his *Jackson,* for he seems never to have sent the manuscript to England. It was finally published by J. B. Lippincott and Company in 1873.

In time of composition the beginning of *Lee* was dovetailed into the end of *Her Majesty the Queen,* and when the life of the general was completed Cooke did not directly commence a new book. He was tired from continuous work, and was worried by the sickness of his son "Eddie," so he wrote a few magazine articles and worked out in his mind the plot of the later romance, *Justin Harley*. He also determined on and began a revision of *The Shadow on the Wall*. On July 20 he sent two hundred pages to Sheffield and Stone of the St. Louis *Home Journal*. As composition proceeded, Cooke grew more and more delighted with the character of Dr. Vandyke, and consequently recalled the introductory chapters from Sheffield and Stone and offered the complete work, finished in December, to Appleton. He had successively referred to the manuscript as *The Bride of the Rivanna* and *At Midnight*, but he readily agreed to *Dr. Vandyke*, the title suggested by Bunce, who intended to publish the work in *Appleton's Journal*. Bunce later gave to a serial by De Mille the space reserved for *Dr. Vandyke*, but offered to print the latter as a volume. The author preferred octavo to the usual duodecimo, and the book appeared in 1872 with numerous full-page illustrations. The titular hero bears a strong resemblance to Dr. Fossyl in *Ellie*. There are, however, few traces of Cooke's antebellum manner. The story is wildly melodramatic. An insane nobleman, believing himself endowed with "second-sight," stabs his wife on the night of his wedding and then commits suicide; two mentally diseased girls are rescued by the skilful doctor from their fearful predicament: one is led out to Christian cheerfulness, the other to happy wifehood. Of such elements as these Cooke fabricates a plot which is typical of his later manner, and owes many incidents to his previous work. The scene of *Dr. Vandyke* is laid in Williamsburg and on the upper James River in late Colonial times. The Virginia names, Bland and Cary, are borne by characters, and reference is made to several famous estates, such as William Byrd's "Westover." The *Virginia Gazette* and the vessel "Charming Sally" are mentioned; but in spite of these superficial local details, the story is not at all a reflection of Virginia life. It is not to be compared with *The Virginia Comedians*, the historical period of which it shares.

The first instalment of *Paul, the Hunter*, the rewritten *Pride of Falling Water*, was sent to the St. Louis *Home Journal* on January 6, 1871, to replace the recalled *Dr. Vandyke*. The work was finished on the third of August. Its scene is laid around Cooke's early haunts; "Glengary" is referred to, and the familiar Wagner of *Fairfax* is once more depicted. Cooke reserved the right to publish the work in volume form, but it was never reprinted.

Before continuing—with *Justin Harley* and *Canolles*—in the field of Colonial times, Cooke wrote a novel of contemporary society on the shore of the Chesapeake. The idea occurred to him on January 23, 1873; work was begun two days later; and the book was finished on February 25. The growing manuscript was successively called *Some Country People, Jack Daintries, The Hollies,* and *Pretty Mrs. Gaston.* Cooke's difficulty in his choice of a title is, as usual, interesting. The one first thought of is too colorless as well as too general. The second is not wholly appropriate, for Daintries is no more important than a half-dozen other characters. *The Hollies* is not altogether to be condemned, for it is the name of Mrs. Gaston's home at which many of the incidents take place. Of the four titles *Pretty Mrs. Gaston* is best, but it has no such definite appropriateness as, for instance, *Tess of the D'Urbervilles*, for the attractive widow is by no means a dominant figure in the book.

Pretty Mrs. Gaston is a pleasant conventional story with a bothersome will, and the rescue of a sweet girl from injury; and it culminates in a number of expected marriages. The book deserves neither praise nor blame. It served its temporary purpose, and is now forgotten. It is mildly diverting, but is of no interest as a record of life and manners, for it is Virginian only by the author's statement. The persons are as conventional as the plot, and the events might have been localized at any spot where English-speaking people congregate. *Pretty Mrs. Gaston* was offered to *Appleton's Journal*, but was declined, the editor politely alleging that serials were not succeeding. It was brought out in 1874 by the Orange Judd Company in an attractively bound duodecimo volume, copiously illustrated with cuts which are not only wretchedly executed, but show the slovenly artist's unfamiliarity with the story. The plump Mrs. Gaston, for instance, is depicted as much leaner than the slender Annie Bell. With *Pretty Mrs. Gaston* were bound two shorter stories, "Annie at the Corner," and "The Wedding at Duluth."

As far back as July 27, 1872, Cooke had been revolving in his head a story of old Virginia which his wife wished him "to call *Cary of Hunsdon*," but which eventually appeared as *Justin Harley*. Still a prey to worry at having followed the style of composition exemplified in *Out of the Foam*, he again "determined to abandon the Reade-Collinsish style of mystery and sensation and come to less spasmodic writing—depending on a 'pleasant' style and characteristic delineation of real life in Va." The latter he regarded as his "true field." "This I began with in the *Comedians* and *St. John*," he says, "and I think any literary individuality and real reputation I have based on my writings in this department." The writing of *Cary of Hunsdon* did not go forward well, and on January 14, 1873, the author made "a highly successful re-beginning of 'Carysbrook.'" Now, however, came the interruption caused by the composition of *Pretty Mrs. Gaston* and, when resumed, the "Cary" story was as difficult as ever. Cooke decided to pattern the hero more or less closely on Harry Warren in the short story, "The Wedding at Duluth," and so far had kept to his idea of making the novel pleasant, descriptive, and historical, rather than sensational. George Cary Eggleston, who spent at "The Briars" the week of August 3, thought, from a perusal of the earlier portion, that the work was of the type of *The Virginia Comedians*, but perhaps superior. Cooke was "quite stirred . . . up" by Eggleston's visit, and "parted with him reluctantly." The publishers of *To-day* (Philadelphia) were, however, "anxiously awaiting" a large instalment of the novel, and Cooke hurried. He soon admittedly fell into sensationalism, but thought *Justin Harley* "tolerably good" in a "bad way." The story was an "immense favorite" with the readers of *To-day* and the publisher followed its serial run with its issue in 1875 in volume form under the imprint of Claxton, Remson & Haffelfinger (Philadelphia). The serial and the book were illustrated. "The illustrations by my friend Sheppard," said Cooke with excellent judgment, "are I must say *atrocious*. He seems not to have the least idea of the text."

Justin Harley begins with a description of certain members of several old Virginia families, but these worthies are soon involved in the meshes of tawdry melodrama. The book not only exemplifies the impossibility of Cooke's going back at this period of his life to the style of *The Virginia Comedians*, but shows vividly how his inventiveness was flagging. The queer-minded Puccoon is Hunter John Myers of *Leather Stocking and Silk*. The Lady of the Snow is an actress, as is Beatrice Hallam. The attractive lowly child proves to be well-born, as in *The Last of the Foresters* and *Ellie*. The lovers take a Browningesque ride, as in *Surry*. The hero believes himself a murderer as in *Mohun*. There is the recovery of a person left supposedly dead, a feature found in *Dr. Vandyke* and *Surry*. Both St. Leger and Harley secure through accident the first embrace of a loved one—a trick common to many of Cooke's books. Mr.

Hicks is Tugmuddle, and the imported Lincolnshire drainage expert is a counterpart of the German gardener in *The Heir of Gaymount*. Many other parallels might be cited. In fact *Justin Harley* looks back for incident through Cooke's whole previous career as a writer of fiction. The novel has, however, a few portraits worthy of appearing in the *Virginia Comedians* gallery. One would like especially to know more of Judge Bland's aged mother who "was a perfect chronicle in herself of every Virginia family," and whose chamber was "drawing-room number two" for all comers to the house.

It has been noted that Cooke, after the war, found the New York *World* immediately hospitable to his contributions, and the Northern press in general ready to receive works from his pen. He did not, however, neglect Southern publications, and sent a number of papers to the Baltimore *New Eclectic* and its successor, the *Southern Magazine*, a brilliant but ephemeral monthly. In March, 1873, George Cary Eggleston wrote Cooke a letter expressing gratitude for encouragement when a young man in ante-bellum Richmond, and asking for contributions to *Hearth and Home*. Cooke replied with some manuscripts and for several years was a frequent contributor to his friend's popular illustrated weekly. Perhaps the most helpful of Cooke's Northern friends was, however, O. B. Bunce of *Appleton's Journal*. From the late sixties well up to the end of the seventies, the Southern writer sent him scores of articles most of which were accepted and paid for promptly. The large amount of periodical literature produced by Cooke during the seventies was, as usual, chiefly of three types, Virginia history, criticism, and sentimental fiction. Cooke did not hesitate to make repeated use of a subject. A short interview with Thackeray during the latter's tour of America resulted in "Thackeray and his 'People,' " "A Talk With

Thackeray," "An Hour With Thackeray," and at least
two other articles. The Virginia novelist found the English-
man "a most excellent genial gentleman and companion."
In a reply to a question Thackeray "smiled in a good-natured way, and said: 'I really don't know where I got
all the rascals in my works. I certainly have never lived
with such people.'"

Cooke seems to have done little in 1874 except write
shorter papers for periodicals; for the early part of the
year was the "hardest year yet, no wheat, no literary returns, nothing but esperance!" By June 27 he had written 450 pages of a novel dealing with the period of the
Revolution and at first called *Dinsmore,* but later given the
name *Cary of Hunsdon,* a discarded title of *Justin Harley.*
Like Thackeray and Dickens, who grieved over the killing
of favorite characters, Cooke said of André: "I am much
concerned about poor André who makes me melancholy."
He determined to send the manuscript to Appleton, Leslie,
and Harper in the order named. Leslie accepted, paying
him $1,000 in four monthly instalments. The work was
never reprinted.

In his next book Cooke continued to use the American
Revolution as a background. *Canolles* was finished on August 4, 1876, was published in the Detroit *Free Press,* and
was brought out in book form in 1877 by Belford Brothers
of Toronto. Canolles, the titular hero, is a Revolutionary
warrior who fights on the American side, but not under
the American flag, and is hence considered an outlaw. His
capture and escape, rides in the swamp, fights, and love
affairs make up the book. Lafayette, Wayne, Tarleton,
and Arnold appear in brief scenes. Like a number of
Cooke's stories, *Canolles* begins with the conventional yet
effective opening, the man on horseback at sunset, and in
other respects seems equally hackneyed—especially to one

who has read all its predecessors. In its love and war adventures it has elements decidedly suggestive of *Surry*; in its free handling of early American history it harks back to *The Virginia Comedians*. Its appearance in print marked the culmination of another stage of Cooke's literary career, for he was never again to produce a novel in the field or in the manner of either of these two important works.

CHAPTER V

LAST YEARS—CONCLUSION

ALTHOUGH John Esten Cooke never experienced an illness serious enough to interrupt for any length of time his literary work, he was, on the contrary, never extremely robust. In the seventies he was afflicted with the neuralgia of the teeth which annoyed him in the fifties, had a yearly attack of hay-fever about September 1, and was troubled by other unpleasant though apparently transitory ailments. "I have had," he recorded in 1877, "an *excruciating* time with rheumatism which racked me day and night."

Before Cooke had been married half a decade, he had begun to be perturbed over the state of his wife's health. In 1873 Mrs. Cooke was badly shaken up by stepping off the porch at "Pagebrook," and in 1875 her husband noted her "lassitude." "Mary is rather pulled down by the weather in spite of cod liver, ale and sherry," he wrote in the summer of 1877. The intermittently composed diary contains the following entry for Cooke's birthday, November 3: "A charming, brilliant day, the perfection of weather to live in—and I am forty-seven! It seems not much, but it is two-thirds of human life—which should make one thoughtful. There is nothing to do, but try to do your duty, love your neighbor, believe and trust in God and our Redeemer and leave the rest to a greater power than any on earth." The autumn and early winter saw the family in good health. Christmas passed with the usual festivities, an abundance of good things to eat, and numerous guests. The tree was

139

especially pretty; it was decorated by Mrs. Cooke, who supplemented the usual features by placing artificial birds on
the boughs. The entry telling of the holiday gaieties closes
with the frequently used and jauntily penned motto, ''Esperance.'' The word, as the journal stands, is crossed out
and by it is written, ''Finis, January 15, 1878.'' This entry,
in his now to be discontinued diary, refers to the sudden
death of his wife.

When Cooke had somewhat recovered from his grief, his
thoughts naturally turned to the future of his motherless
children. He left them at ''Saratoga,'' the home of their
uncle, Powel Page, and journeyed to the Tidewater region
of Virginia to pay a visit to his sister Sal at ''Orapax'' in
New Kent County. Here he not only received mental com-
fort, but returned home accompanied by Miss Mariah Pendleton Duval, his sister's eldest daughter, who for a while
directed the education and upbringing of his children.
Much as she loved her uncle's children, the gifted Miss
Duval could not, of course, sacrifice a career to their service. The author's decision, therefore, was to keep his
sons at home while he entrusted his daughter to her mother's
sister, Mrs. William Carter of ''The Glen.'' The boys also
paid frequent and extended visits to the house of their aunt,
and thus ''The Briars'' was no longer the scene of the busy
social activity which it had witnessed under its gracious
mistress.

The novelist is, in fact, described by many of his friends
as having been a rather lonely figure during his widowed
years. Miss Duval has given an excellent account of his
life at this period. The stone mansion-house of ''The
Briars'' was built in the form of an ''L.'' On the right of
the entrance was a spacious parlor lighted by four large
windows with solid wooden shutters. The furniture of this
room was old and quaint, and portraits of Cooke's parents

shared the wall-space with Confederate souvenirs among which was the coat that had once been Stuart's. The bereaved novelist daily placed a fresh flower in a vase before the portrait of his wife which occupied the place of honor above the mantel. The parlor was, in the words of Miss Duval, "the abiding-place" of the writer. In a big leather chair to the left of the hearth he would lead morning prayer, carry on conversation, or often sit in silent thought, his fingers placed tip to tip while his elbows rested on the arms of the chair. At table the novelist sat with a son at either side. The family always enjoyed right royal meals. One Christmas, for instance, the "very pleasant dinner" consisted of "ham (old), roast turkey, beefsteak, chine and cabbage, oyster soup, sherry, plum pudding, jelly, salsify, etc."

After breakfast Cooke would normally devote himself to his literary projects. Usually, amid a cloud of smoke from a meerschaum of whose color he was very proud, he wrote nervously from nine until two, and could tolerate no interruption. Even the tapping of a dog's tail upon the floor is said to have annoyed him. In this seclusion he produced copy with great rapidity, though he naturally proceeded more carefully with books like his *Virginia*. In spite of the recommendation of a Northern friend, he never adopted the use of a typewriter, but to the end of his life his manuscript continued pleasant to look at and easy to read. Before his wife's death Cooke had made a practice of showing her his work as he composed it. She was not a thorough-going critic, but was often helpful, for instance in advising against the insertion in *Her Majesty the Queen* of one of Susie's baby songs. After his wife's death he often sought the critical judgment of his niece. His sister Sal, the member of his family with the best critical acumen, was unfortunately rarely near him.

At two o'clock Cooke's working day was over. The afternoons and, sometimes, the mornings, were given to the management of the farm and to odd jobs in the lawn or the garden. At four o'clock the family carriage always stood at the door for the daily drive to Millwood, the post office, five miles away; and the novelist, when he made the trip, would indulge in friendly chats with the occupants of other vehicles. In addition to the immediate family of himself and his wife, Cooke had many friends in the neighborhood. Notable among them was the "humorous, bright and happy" Mr. John Page of the nearby estate, "Longwood." Twilight would often find either the Cookes walking across the fields toward his home, or him and his two daughters approaching "The Briars." Other friends were Captain William Nelson of "Linden," Captain William Carter of "The Glen," and Judge John Evelyn Page of "Pagebrook" —all three of whom were men of literary taste and culture. In the congenial atmosphere afforded by an occasional exchange of visits with these and other acquaintances, Cooke carried forward his career as a man of letters.

In the spring following the death of his wife Cooke again visited New York. Here he became for the first time familiar with the phonograph, and was profoundly impressed by it. He regretted to the end of his life that he had not preserved a record of his wife's voice which he always thought very beautiful and described as that of May Beverley in *Surry of Eagle's-Nest*. The contemplation of the new scientific marvel, together with the serious thought induced by the death of his wife, led him to write a novelette entitled *Professor Pressensee, Materialist and Inventor*. The story is told in the first person. The narrator recounts that in New York, in 1872, he "spends an evening at the Century Club, the resort of authors, artists and others of similar tastes." Here he sees a Professor

Pressensee and on the way back to the hotel helps protect him from three thugs who are trying to garrote him. Rescuer and rescued become acquainted and the materialist professor asks the narrator to speak into the "phonometer": "I would test his wonderful machine; but what should I say to it? I was not in a mood to whisper to it some inane jest; I was indeed the farthest possible from mirth. Revolted by the fearful materialism of the inventor, I placed my mouth as he directed, and said deliberately, 'You assert, Professor Pressensee, that there is no personal Deity—that God is matter, and matter is God; and Heat is the persistent Force creating all things. You utter a philosophic heresy. Behind Heat is Law, behind Law is the Absolute: this Absolute is the central Soul of the universe, in whose spiritual image you and I are made—the living God—before whom we will stand with all human beings we have loved or hated, to answer for the deeds done in the body.' " Pressensee's answer is quoted on the title-page of the book: " 'I am Pressensee. I stand on that. Who or what made me I don't know. I do not believe in your future state, or your Absolute Soul. Man and the worm are the same. There is no *Life* after *Death*. Life is heat. Heat goes and death comes—that is all I know about it. Witness my hand and seal, Pressensee."

The narrator leaves New York and two years later on a recuperating trip through the Virginia mountains is surprised to discover Pressensee and his daughter. The professor has lost his wife and is very much reduced in health. He has refused to allow his daughter to receive attentions from Henry Alford, a wealthy and manly young New Yorker who has followed them to Virginia and dwells in a cabin in the mountains. The young lady gets her feet wet and nearly dies of typhoid pneumonia, but rallies when her father, upon the advice of the narrator, allows Alford

to see her. The old scientist has already passed from total
atheism to a belief in a vindictive God, and actually prays
at the crisis of his daughter's illness. After a few years
the narrator again crosses the path of the Pressensee family.
The lovers are now married and have two children, and
the inventor, at last a believer in God, is devoting his time
to the improvement of plows and harvesting machines.
The novelette can perhaps be best described as colorless if
not insipid. It has few of the qualities of a well-told story,
and is weak as a piece of Christian propaganda, since the
reasons for Pressensee's assumption of faith are not made
apparent. *Professor Pressensee* was published promptly
(1878) in Harper's *Half-Hour Series*—a collection of small,
thin volumes which retailed at from fifteen to twenty-five
cents in paper covers or at fifteen cents additional in cloth.

Cooke's next work of fiction of book length was a novelette somewhat of the type of *Professor Pressensee*. Like its
predecessor, *Mr. Grantley's Idea* appeared in the distinguished company afforded by the *Half-Hour Series*, and
marked another point scored in the author's effort to break
away from the melodramatic tendency that so thoroughly
mastered him in the earlier seventies. The plot is not
wholly a new one to Cooke, but shows a trend toward originality. A boy snatches a necklace from a little girl, is
caught by Higgins, the jailer, and is carried before the
girl's father, a magistrate. The latter is about to sentence
the culprit to be whipped, but the boy's despair at his anticipated disgrace leads the girl to plead for him. The girl's
father, Mr. Heath, then imposes the minimum sentence—
three days in jail on a bread and water diet. The boy, on
the way to jail riding horseback behind Higgins, strikes
him suddenly on the face, and effects an escape. In his
haste he bruises his bare feet on the stones in the road and
is taken into a carriage by a kindly Episcopalian bishop who

happens to be passing. Ten or twelve years later a young
pastor is called to the village where the Heaths live and
dwells with them while the parsonage is being repaired.
The new minister is Mr. Grantley, formerly the boy rogue.
In carrying out his "idea" he preaches his first sermon on
the text, "Thou shalt not steal," and goes quietly to jail,
where he remains three days. Finally he discovers that he
loves Rose Heath, and is about to leave his charge, when, in
an accidental meeting, he tells her his story. Rose says she
loves him, draws closer to him, leans her head upon his
breast, and speaks, "Can a husband steal from—his wife?"
This ending would seem very unlike Cooke were it not for
the typical explanation that the boy rogue is really the son
of a Mr. Calvert Grantley, a very dear early friend of Mr.
Heath.

The real advance Cooke achieved in *Mr. Grantley's Idea*
was in the portrayal of rural life in Virginia. He gives
a vivid picture of a chattering crowd around the church-
door on Sunday. The practice "was not wrong. Bishop
Meade had not disapproved of it. He had said, 'Oh, there
is no harm in it. They are all related to each other, and
many families only see each other on Sunday.' " "The
Parish of B—— Becomes Excited" is an excellent chapter
filled with gentle realistic satire directed perhaps at the
Clarke village of Boyce. If the standard here set had been
maintained by the entire book, the novelette might have been
as permanent as some of its famous associates in *The
Half-Hour Series*. True to rural Virginia custom is the
following account of the arrival of the minister and of the
lawn-party designed to yield certain needed funds:

"When the ladies of B—— parish heard that a new minister was
coming they fell into a flutter of curiosity and excitement. There
is something in the ministerial office which attracts their sex. The
person holding it is necessarily better and more intellectual than

other people. When he is young, he is all the more interesting and must be looked after.

"As to Mr. Grantley, he was said to be young, low-church in his views, and an excellent preacher. One or two of the ladies of the congregation had heard him preach in Richmond, and were rapturous about him; he was so eloquent and fine-looking. This was dangerous. The new rector was beginning under disadvantages.

"In a material point of view, the good looks, youth, and eloquence seemed about to prove an advantage. The ladies were going to take the young Timothy under their wing. They were much agitated. There was an animated discussion at a tea-drinking as to the color of his hair. Was he married? There was a determination to give him a cordial reception.

"Excitement requires a safety-valve. This was supplied by the dilapidated condition of the parsonage. . . .

". . . It would not do to have the new rector find the parsonage so dilapidated. He had no children to protect from the leaks, but his eyes might be put out by the smoke while he was composing his sermons. Then the staircase might fall beneath him, and he might break his neck, which would be frightful. . . .

"The parish was poor, the worthy people having little or nothing besides food for their families. They had been very well-off indeed once, but the war had changed things. . . . It thus seemed impossible to raise money for repairs, and it was gained in a very short time. The ladies knew. There was a fair, a bazaar, a raffle, a series of tableaux, some private-public theatricals, and other devices were resorted to. Of course, the theatre, as an institution, was unutterably depraved, but this was quite innocent; and as to the raffling, that was strictly pious—it was not gambling at all, considering the object in view; and taking five-dollar notes in payment for single cigars was perfectly honest—it was for the church.

"By such nefarious and strictly moral means the ladies soon found themselves in possession of a considerable little sum of money."

As early as 1872, Cooke contemplated writing a work to be called "The Virginia Sketch-Book." He referred to this project in 1873 and in 1881, but nothing came of it. To the June, 1876, *Harper's*, however, he contributed a long illustrated article entitled "Virginia in the Revolution."

The Harpers paid Cooke one hundred and fifty dollars for this article, and were evidently pleased with its reception by the public, for in 1878 they asked the author to prepare, for issue in volume form, a series of stories from Virginia history. For this work Cooke was offered only two hundred dollars, but, between his encyclopedia articles and his semi-historical novels, he was already familiar with the field and he accepted the commission. *Stories of the Old Dominion* was published in 1879 as a handsome, profusely illustrated octavo volume. The twenty-one stories, beginning with "The Adventures of Captain John Smith" and concluding with "The Surrender at Yorktown," cover the more dramatic episodes of Virginia history in the Colonial and Revolutionary periods, and are entertainingly told. When not true to facts, they are true to tradition, and show Cooke to have achieved his desire of doing a serious and valuable piece of work. The prologue, "About my Stories," and the impressive epilogue, "A Last Word to the Boys," indicate specifically the character of the book which was dedicated to the author's two sons. Cooke's style was always clear and direct, but here he made a special effort to be "simple." The unnecessary pains resulted in no greater cramping of his style than an occasional superfluous explanation of an easy term, such as: "It was proclaimed on coins, that is, pieces of money." A few defects of this nature do not, however, obscure the merit of a book some of whose chapters are charming as well as vigorous. Perhaps it was no hard task to give the flavor of romance to the story of Captain John Smith; but other figures are as effectively handled. Very vivid is the picture of Daniel Morgan, who built his family seat with the labor of the hated Hessians and said in old age: "To be young once more. . . . I would be willing to be stripped naked and hunted through the Blue Ridge with wild dogs." The purpose of Cooke's work was admirable; he wished to make great and good men of the young Virginians who read it. The inspirational epilogue may well have influenced his younger son who, in Walter Reed's yellow fever experiments in Cuba, offered his life with as much bravery as any ancestor had ever shown in facing a human enemy.

Cooke's next book, *The Virginia Bohemians,* was a long novel which was published by the Harpers in 1880. It was in its conception another serious effort at producing a work of value. It includes elements from its fictional next older brother, *Mr. Grantley's Idea,* but can best be described as a hybrid partaking of the nature of *The Virginia Comedians* on one hand and *The Heir of Gaymount* on the other. For true local color, *The Virginia Bohemians* holds primacy among Cooke's novels. The name Bohemia, given to a mountain valley, was perhaps suggested by "Arabia," the actual name of such a valley in Clarke County. Across the Blue Ridge from Bohemia lies—in the story—the little village of Piedmont. Piedmont, of course, is the name of a broad belt through Virginia, and the village is intended to be typical. The two churches, the town pump, the blacksmith shop with the crowd of small boys, the village store with a porch full of idlers awaiting the stage—all these are excellently presented, especially in the chapter entitled "Piedmont wakes up." This part of the novel is of "photographic accuracy to Virginia life," as Margaret Junkin Preston described it. Of nearly equal merit is Cooke's description of the circus and its effect on Piedmont. Here, however, he exhibits a habit which is one of the main characteristics of another Southern writer, Mrs. Augusta Evans Wilson: he parades his learning in numerous literary and historical allusions and in the use of foreign and unanglicized words. In a single short paragraph, for example, there are a half-dozen allusions, and "aura," "populus," "ennui," and "élite," appear. Of the plot, nothing need be said save that it inclines to Cooke's more complicated type and fails to share the freshness of the setting. There are mountaineers and impoverished aristocrats, sweet young girls and an adventuress, a New Yorker, old soldiers, a few negroes of the household servant class, and a gallery of circus people. The chapter entitled "The Old Chapel" is Cooke's effort to give the immortality of print to a beloved old church in Clarke. Ellis Grantham suggests Mr. Grantley of *Mr. Grantley's Idea,* and is probably Cooke's portrait of the ideal minister. General Lascelles is an excellent portrait; there were many of the type in Virginia. The old general is always glad to have a guest in his study so that if he wishes "to ejaculate denunciations connected with contemporary politics," they may be heard. The Big Monopoly Railroad is attacked as the cause of low prices of farm produce and such sentences as the following are inserted: "Crossing the big white Chester and the small black Essex, he produced a species like the Berkshire, which he said was the best hog of all." Such observations of course give tedium to the plot; but, on the other hand, serve to fill out Cooke's picture of the Virginia of 1880.

The usually unfavorable opinion of the Boston critics, some of whose hostile criticism Cooke consolidated in the preface to *Hilt to Hilt,* did not prevent Houghton, Mifflin and Company from recognizing the substantial merit of the Southern author. Cooke was asked to write the history of Virginia for the "American Commonwealths" series, edited by Horace E. Scudder. He spent more time on this history than on any book he ever wrote and must have taken delight in going systematically through the older histories and other sources, and refreshing his mind on the facts and legends which had charmed him from boyhood. Much of the matter from *Stories of the Old Dominion* is of course repeated in *Virginia; A History of the People,* but the composition of the previous work did not unduly influence the latter, as any random comparison will show. With only about thirty-five of over five hundred pages devoted to the years since 1800, *Virginia* is strictly a history of Colonial Virginia and the state's part in founding the nation. For the first two centuries of Virginia history, however, Cooke's volume is an excellent manual, accurate enough for the ordinary reader and intensely interesting. The author preserves a fine balance between the sweeping events of war at one extreme and the depiction of the quiet life of the people at the other, and, without a vigilant regard for the whole truth, succeeds, like Macaulay, in giving to history the glamor of fiction.

Upon its appearance in 1883, *Virginia* commanded wide and favorable attention. The New York *Critic* spoke of its "interest," and its "earnest desire to do all parties and religions perfect justice." The New York *Times* was hostile, but the new work was praised by the *Evening Post* and the *Sun.* The latter was especially complimentary: "It would be not easy to speak of this performance in terms of too hearty commendation. There is no man of letters in this country so manifestly qualified for the task here undertaken, and it would have been almost impertinent to have selected any other." On February 4, 1884, Stedman wrote Cooke a very interesting letter, urging a visit to New York, and giving an opinion of *Virginia.* "You would have done well to use less of the 'animated present tense,'" he said; but otherwise he liked the history. "The narrative is clear, synthetic, fluent, and vivid in every way; Virginians and all other Americans owe you a debt for this graceful and scholarly work."

The chapter on "Virginia Literature in the Nineteenth Century" lists a number of books and writers and affords an insight into the literary views of Cooke who concludes: "Whatever may be the true rank of the literature, it possesses a distinct character. It may be said of it with truth that it is nowhere offensive to delicacy or piety; or endeavors to instill a belief in what ought not to be believed. It is a very great deal to say of the literature of any country in the nineteenth century." Although it failed to achieve the spectacular initial success of *Surry of Eagle's-Nest*, *Virginia* has had the steadiest sale of any of Cooke's books. To the edition of 1903, there was added a supplementary chapter by William G. Brown; and by 1915 thirty impressions all told had been printed and approximately thirteen thousand copies had been sold.

Cooke relieved the strain of his arduous work on *Virginia* by the composition of *Fanchette* which appeared in 1883, a few months ahead of the history. The novel was issued by James R. Osgood and Company of Boston in the anonymous Round-Robin series. Around a device on the title-page, the books of this series carried the motto "Perhaps it may turn out a song, Perhaps turn out a sermon." *Fanchette* is neither a sermon nor a song, but a very melodramatic tale which owes a part of its plot to *The Virginia Comedians*, the master work to which Cooke so often turned when the candle of his inspiration was dim or flickering. Like Beatrice, Fanchette hates the stage, goes about with the actor who fathered her when she was orphaned, and marries the serious person who performs a heroic rescue. The plot of *Fanchette* is complicated, and in one respect repulsive. Detail after detail leads the reader to suspect that Armyn is Fanchette's father, and their marriage comes as a distinct shock. Cooke begins the story with a view of Washington life in the summer of the year of a Presidential election, presumably that of 1880, but in short order introduces a ruined Russian prince, an oriental prophet, a lady in a tower, and a Rajah of Kabul. One is reminded of *The Heir of Gaymount* where buried treasure crept into what purported to be an economic study. Cooke's views on contemporary fiction are aired in a conversation between the cultivated middle-aged Waring and the ebullient Armyn. Armyn reads "a good deal of light literature—it is a rest; rarely novels." Waring ironically assures him that he is missing "the dissection of souls, the analysis of the human heart." *Fanchette* is not in any sense a notable story; but it shows the development of Cooke's character. A bereaved man speaks more than once in an unobtrusive passage in the frequently subjective *Stories of the Old Dominion*, and in *Fanchette* there is occasionally a personal note. The author was doubtless thinking of his dead wife when he wrote passages like the following: "Given a gallant young company, and a cloudless sky, life is always gay. It is only when the sun goes down, and the gray-beard at the helm hears the moan of the sea, that he thinks of the unknown port to which he is steering." In *Fanchette* Cooke has more than his usual number of arresting sentences. His style seems pithier. It was perhaps benefited by the thoughtful attention given to the history of Virginia.

As early as 1859 Thomas Dunn English, writing to Cooke relative to a proposed lecturing tour in which they should "hunt in couples" or "drive tandem," suggested that the Virginia novelist write a story with one of Captain John Smith's men as the hero. Ten years later English again suggested the subject, this time in more detail. "There is," he wrote, "one subject for you, which you have not touched—for the reason that a man rarely knows the most fertile field to cultivate. When you do touch it, you will make a success. I mean the early settlement of the Old Dominion. When you make up your mind to trot out Captain John Smith as a hero, and Pocahontas as a heroine,

let me know, and I will furnish you with some data acces-
sible enough here, but out of your reach in your region.
A good long novel of that period is a desideratum—and you
are the man to do it. It's an opportune time, too. The
public are growing tired of society novels, war stories and
criminal romances.''

With this encouragement and his fondness for Colonial
Virginia, it is surprising that Cooke did not sooner weave a
romance around the settlement at Jamestown. At last,
however, he wrote *My Lady Pokahontas*, and it was published by Houghton, Mifflin and Company early in 1885.
As in *The Virginia Comedians* and *Surry of Eagle's-Nest*,
Cooke does not tell the story directly, but merely furnishes
"notes" to a "True Relation of Virginia, Writ by Anas
Todkill, Puritan and Pilgrim.'' True to its pretence of
being a document of the early seventeenth century, the work
is studded with certain linguistic archaisms, but the style is
essentially modern in its grace, simplicity, and cleverness.
Cooke once thought of writing a series of tales localized in
the Mermaid Tavern, and in *My Lady Pokahontas* he introduces that famous hostelry. As in *Her Majesty the Queen*,
he makes his quota of allusions. Shakespeare is mentioned
repeatedly, and Todkill states the "fact" that "Master
Shakespeare'' made "his strange Caliban'' of Rawhunt, a
dwarf henchman of Powhatan, and "his Miranda'' of
Pocahontas. Cooke's story is agreeable but is practically
devoid of plot apart from the love of Pocahontas and Smith,
and the Indian girl's transfer of her affection when she
is convinced that the famous captain is dead. *My Lady
Pokahontas* occupies a prominent place in the long list [1] of
novels, plays, and poems which deal with its titular heroine.

---

[1] The Pocahontas story is thoroughly discussed in Mr. Jay B.
Hubbell's fascinating and scholarly forthcoming work, *Virginia Life
in Fiction*.

Master Anas's reminiscences are, however, far too tenuous to be the great novel for which Thomas Dunn English had hoped.

Later in 1885 Cooke's last book, *The Maurice Mystery*, was brought out by D. Appleton and Company. The scene of the novel is laid "in what is called the Piedmont region —that is to say, the eastern slope of the long range of mountains extending from Maryland to Northern Georgia." The time is 1880, but the "mystery" goes back to 1860 when a murder was committed at "Mauricewood," an old family seat. The interest of the book is divided between the Cary-Haworth love affair and the discovery of the murderer, the plot suggesting Bulwer-Lytton's *Devereux*. *The Maurice Mystery* contains many reflections of the author's personality.   Cooke discusses life after death—a problem that seems to have obsessed him after the loss of his wife. He refers to Pontmartin, Browning, and other writers in whom he was interested.   French and Latin phrases are printed with typographical errors.   Romance is sought by including among the characters an opium fiend and some adventurers who have lived in South America.   Such well-worn tricks as concealed identity and mutilated records are again made use of.   Despite its background in the Piedmont region of the South, the novel has no local color.   It was reprinted by the G. W. Dillingham Company, but has slight claim to continued life.

In the eighties Cook continued writing for periodicals. True to his democratic instinct he wrote occasionally throughout his life unpaid-for pieces for the local weeklies of Clarke and other counties.   Just as he might have handed around to guests a basket of the fruit which he was selling, so he let his literary talent serve his neighbors as well as earn him a livelihood.   He now produced less poetry than before the war, but it was of the same type, fluent, unpolished, trite. He always wished to visit England, and in later life became intimate with several English families in the county of Fauquier. As a compliment to these friends, he wrote "A Sigh for England;" but neither subject nor occasion inspired him to a very distinguished composition:

A SIGH FOR ENGLAND

If I could choose this golden morn
  Of summer when the days are long,
My music, I would listen to
  The English skylark's song.

If I could see what more than all
  In the wide world I long to see,
Give me the English sunshine dashed
  On castle, tower or tree.

Only to tread where Shakespeare trod,
  Only to see the daisies grow,
Only to hear, in English trees,
  The wind's talk, soft and low.

But swiftly fly the passing years,
  And all is but a dream at best;
I dream of the dear English fields
  To waken in the West.

In his later years Cooke wrote less frequently for the New York and other Eastern publications. On the contrary he contributed frequently to the Detroit *Free Press* and the *Southern World*. He produced, as usual, stories, serials, and articles; but was, for new bodies of readers, largely working over his old productions. Even in his contributions to *Harper's* his loss of originality was striking. "The Writer of the Declaration of Independence; A Familiar Sketch" is, for instance, a reworking of the data given in the appendix to *The Youth of Jefferson,* and also owes something to Cooke's encyclopedia article on Jefferson. Of the stories "The Craniologist" and "Owlet" may be noticed. The former reflects the interest in science and philosophy which was characteristic of the author's later life. The latter shows how Cooke in a short story combined certain incidents of his experience with the conventional ingredients of his later novels. A young lawyer of "R——," tired from "confinement and overwork" during the summer, sets out on horseback for the Valley of Virginia where he has "a number of hospitable and warm-hearted relations." On his journey the narrator stops at the cabin of Daddy Bayne and there meets "Owlet," a pretty but wholly untaught girl. Later "Owlet" is taken into the home of the narrator's aunt. She receives polish rapidly, proves to be an English heiress, and is married to the man who discovered her at Daddy Bayne's.

The last years of Cooke's life were uneventful. An occasional visit to New York and the companionship of friends were the chief diversions from his settled routine. In his pleasant home he was proud of his children who, as he justly thought, were growing up with honor to their ancestry. The author regularly attended Christ Church at Millwood. Here, with his boys, he occupied the family pew, and the three reverently took part in the service. After the exercises Cooke would indulge in a neighborly chat with other worshipers, and would often go for dinner with Dr. C. Braxton Bryan at the rectory, or with other friends in the vicinity.

In the summer of 1886 Cooke's sister Sal was with him. He was working on a novel destined for the Detroit *Free Press,* but *Dr. Favart's Strange Experiences* was never completed. Although the author toward the end of September became feeble and languid, neither he nor his family realized how ill he was until he fainted in his chair. A physician was summoned, but for three days Cooke persisted in an effort to throw off his illness. At last he could resist no longer; he yielded to his malady which was typhoid fever, and, very ill indeed, was put to bed. He died the next day, September 27, 1886. He was laid to rest beside his wife, and near two of his brothers, in the Old Chapel burying-ground. In memory of his brilliant nephews, the last of whom he survived by nearly a decade, General Philip St. George Cooke presented to the Millwood Church a stained-glass window. The lily in this window has a dual significance. It refers to the descent of the Cookes from the Esten family of Bermuda, and at the same time symbolizes the peace that at length came to a family torn asunder by the Civil War.

Little need be said of Cooke the man. His only surviving son, Robert, once wrote to his sister that they had more right to be proud of their father's Christian character than of his literary fame. This is certainly true. Whatever may be said of Cooke's talent as a writer, his character is above reproach. Thousands of pages of letters and other personal manuscripts contain not the slightest suggestion that he was ever inspired by any save the highest motives. "Time had wrought no change in his nature," said George Cary Eggleston. "He remained to the end the high-spirited, duty-loving man of honor that I had known in my youth; he remained also the gentle, affectionate and unfailingly courteous gentleman he had always been." Cooke was as pure and honorable in his life as he strove to be in his books. He was from first to last a democrat, a gentleman, and a Christian in the best sense of each word.

Although Cooke's death was widely noted, it resulted in no serious estimates of his career, and probably did not impress the literary world as much as it would have done

had it occurred in 1859 or in 1867. In the former year
he was not yet thirty, but was a leader in the *Southern
Literary Messenger* group of writers, and had made an important contribution to the literature of his native state.
In the latter year he was at the apex of his success as a
writer of Civil War stories with a Southern bias. Despite
the merit of his historical work in the eighties, Cooke did
not keep as fully in the public eye as he had done. In his
seclusion at ''The Briars'' he lacked vigorous intellectual
stimulus. By the time of his death his name was being
crowded out of the better magazines by younger writers,
who were more careful if not more talented.

Cooke has now been dead a third of a century and it is
time for some estimate to be placed on his work. First of
all, it should be said that he was not a great literary genius
and neither claimed nor thought he was. He always referred to his talent as less than that of his eldest brother,
and his judgment was correct. Philip Pendleton Cooke was
an ill-starred genius, comparable in many ways to Edgar
Allan Poe. When he died at the age of thirty-three he had
produced but one book. In striking contrast, John Esten
Cooke was enormously prolific. In an active career of little
more than three decades he served through the Civil War,
devoted himself in his later years to the management of a
farm, and yet produced thirty books, together with an
amount of fugitive matter which would fill at least fifteen
volumes. Cooke's fluency was the cause of his chief faults.
He wrote far too rapidly for his training and talents.
Unlike Philip, he had not received a university education,
and the want of it is seen in much that he wrote. He dis-
liked revision, and consequently shows an occasional irreg-
ular sentence. He produced contiguous passages and contiguous chapters of vastly unequal merit. He was weak
in invention; many incidents in his later works are copied

from some earlier production. He failed to adapt his characters to his setting. His world-traveled, melodramatic heroes and villains are out of place in a Virginia background. Most of his female characters are of one pattern and are particularly weak. They are described as delicate, sprightly "little beauties," but to the reader they appear immature and colorless. Throughout his career Cooke made the mistake of writing on subjects with which he was not wholly familiar. According to his lights, however, his justification is complete. Under no disillusion in regard to his genius, he would turn from one species of composition to another, as a farmer might change his crops, with the idea of financial profit. In his later years his worst work paid best. This seeming anomaly encouraged a natural taste for sentimentality and sensationalism and shut him off from achieving his finer possibilities. Dr. C. Braxton Bryan bears testimony to the fact that the author more than once said, "I have been obliged to stop what I was doing and write something for checks." Cooke, nevertheless, achieved more than a modicum of distinction. His style is uniformly clear and agreeable. He usually had an eye for the picturesque. His movement is rapid and his dialogue is normally true to life. In everything he wrote, there is an element of sprightliness, dash, and manliness. Cooke was a gentleman-romancer who wrote while the spell of composition was upon him and devoted himself to his family and friends instead of revising his manuscript.

In spite of the fairly brief span of his life, Cooke was undoubtedly the most representative Virginian who has ever earned a livelihood by writing. Born in 1830 in what is now West Virginia, he knew, almost at first hand, the Colonial border. He lived in the Richmond of the fifties. He saw the full stress of the Civil War. Later as a fairly well-to-do farmer he shared the position of thousands of modern Virginians.

Cooke was not only a typical Virginia writer, but no other before or since has given such whole-hearted devotion to the service of the Old Dominion. In his *Stories of the Old Dominion* and *Virginia* he swept the history of the state from 1607 to 1800, and in his fiction he made use of early colonial, late colonial, Revolutionary, ante-bellum, civil war, and post-bellum settings. He chose for his background the border as well as the capital; and, throughout all his works, his spirit toward his native state was one of loyalty and love. When the present seemed sordid in 1850, he sought romance in the past. When Virginia was faced with disaster in the dark days following the Civil War he sought, in his way, to help solve her problems.

On the whole, however, Cooke was not so much the advocate, as the social historian, of Virginia. "My aim," he wrote, "has been to paint the Virginia phase of American society, to do for the Old Dominion what Cooper has done for the Indians, Simms for the Revolutionary drama in South Carolina, Irving for the Dutch Knickerbockers, and Hawthorne for the weird Puritan life of New England." In this worthy ambition Cooke was more than partially successful. His pictures of older Virginia, inaccurate as they may be in minor details, have been accepted by such modern writers as Thomas Nelson Page. His histories and biographies greatly influenced the Susan Pendleton Lee histories of the United States which have secured an immense circulation through their use in Southern public schools. Cooke in fact, partly through his own books but more particularly through his influence, is responsible for the idea of older Virginia held by the Virginians of today.

Cooke is not only intrinsically important as a typical and influential Virginia writer, but is a definite link in the

development of literature pertaining to Virginia. His ultimate literary ancestor was Scott, whose works were read to
him in childhood, and he is a younger brother of Simms.
William Alexander Caruthers, who was writing during
Cooke's boyhood, was his immediate predecessor as a historical novelist of Virginia. The influence of these writers
can, however, be easily exaggerated. Cooke shared their
general purpose rather than imitated any particular book
or method. He, in turn, has handed down the tradition—
especially to Miss Mary Johnston and Mrs. Burton Harrison. *The Long Roll* and *Cease Firing* invite comparison
with *Surry* and *Mohun*, just as *Flower de Hundred* in its
very title recalls *Henry St. John.*

In the eighties Cooke was an exponent of the same type
of novel he wrote in the fifties. An *apologia*, written a
short while before his death, has been widely published:
''I still write stories for such periodicals as are inclined to
accept romance, but whether any more of my work in that
field will appear in book-form is uncertain. Mr. Howells
and the other realists have crowded me out of popular
regard as a novelist, and have brought the kind of fiction
I write into general disfavor. I do not complain of that,
for they are right. They see, as I do, that fiction should
faithfully reflect life, and they obey the law, while I cannot. I was born too soon, and am now too old to learn
my trade anew. But in literature, as in everything else,
advance should be the law, and he who stands still has no
right to complain if he is left behind. Besides, the fires
of ambition are burned out of me, and I am serenely happy.
My wheat-fields are green as I look out from the porch of
'The Briars,' the corn rustles in the wind, and the great
trees give me shade upon the lawn. My three children are
growing up in such nurture and admonition as their race
has always deemed fit, and I am not only content, but very

happy, and much too lazy to entertain any other feeling toward my victors than one of warm friendship and sincere approval.'' Strange as it may seem, the very fact that Cooke had never discarded the romantic tradition, led him to be regarded as a pioneer in the romantic revival which was headed by Stevenson.

In concluding, an answer should perhaps be made to the hypothetical question, what is the status of John Esten Cooke in 1922? Professor Pattee, a leading historian of recent American literature, rates Cooke as ''the best novelist the South produced during the earlier period.'' It must be admitted, nevertheless, that to most Americans Cooke is either unknown or, at most, a name. A few Northerners and a goodly number of Southerners, have, however, read *Surry of Eagle's-Nest*, and perhaps *Mohun* and *Hilt to Hilt*. Others have read one or both of the military biographies. In the six months ending April 30, 1914, ninety-two copies of *Virginia* and thirty-two copies of *My Lady Pokahontas* were sold. At the same time fourteen volumes, in the form of cheap reprints, were on sale by the G. W. Dillingham Company. The recent failure of this house has practically put an end to the sale of Cooke's books, but will help his future reputation. On the Dillingham list he was in poorer company than he deserved, and was brought into disfavor by an ungrammatical, inaccurate, widely circulated advertisement.

A thoroughly impartial appraisal of Cooke results in a protest against his being wholly forgotten. The question then arises, what should be salvaged from an abundance threatened with oblivion? Cooke's poetry is not of enduring value; his faults are unduly conspicuous in his shorter prose articles; and his lives of Lee and Jackson have already been superseded. In spite of their excellence, *Virginia* and *Stories of the Old Dominion* must inevitably await the fate of the biographies. The choice is then narrowed down to the novels. Perhaps a half-score of these deserve to live. The two volumes of *The Virginia Comedians, Surry,* and *Mohun* should by all means be kept continually available for American readers. The first is Cooke's best novel; it is a sweeping portrayal of a field he knew and loved when he was not yet tired from overproduction. *Surry* and *Mohun* were his most popular books, and are still his best remembered works. They contain an essential record of his personal Civil War experience, and give almost as well as the biographies his impressions of the great generals. These two novels—compounded as they are of history, adventure, and idealism—are furthermore of a type well adapted to the youthful readers of the future. Cooke, it would seem in conclusion, will be remembered chiefly for *The Virginia Comedians, Surry of Eagle's-Nest,* and *Mohun.* With these four volumes saved from oblivion, he will continue to be known as a social historian of late Colonial Virginia, and as a romantic Confederate captain, who used his military experience as the basis of fiction.

BIBLIOGRAPHY

BOOKS

In the text subtitles have been given and important later editions have been discussed.

1. 1854. Leather Stocking and Silk. New York: Harper and Brothers.
2, 3. 1854. The Virginia Comedians. (2 vols.) New York: D. Appleton and Company.
4. 1854. The Youth of Jefferson. New York: Redfield.
5. 1855. Ellie. Richmond: A. Morris.
6. 1856. The Last of the Foresters. New York: Derby and Jackson.
7. 1859. Henry St. John, Gentleman. New York: Harper and Brothers.
8. 1863. The Life of Stonewall Jackson. Richmond: Ayres and Wade.
9. 1866. Stonewall Jackson: A Military Biography. New York: D. Appleton and Company.
10. 1866. Surry of Eagles'-Nest. New York: Bunce and Huntington.
11. 1867. Wearing of the Gray. New York: E. B. Treat and Company.
12. 1868. Fairfax. New York: G. W. Carleton and Company.
13. 1869. Hilt to Hilt. New York: G. W. Carleton and Company.
14. 1869. Mohun. New York: F. J. Huntington and Company.
15. 1870. Hammer and Rapier. New York: Carleton.
16. 1870. The Heir of Gaymount. New York: Van Evrie, Horton and Company.
17. 1871. A Life of Gen. Robert E. Lee. New York: D. Appleton and Company.

BIBLIOGRAPHY 165

18. 1872. Out of the Foam. New York: G. W. Carleton and Company.
19. 1872. Dr. Vandyke. New York: D. Appleton and Company.
20. 1873. Her Majesty the Queen. Philadelphia: J. B. Lippincott and Company.
21. 1874. Pretty Mrs. Gaston, and other stories. New York: Orange Judd Company.
22. 1875. Justin Harley. Philadelphia: Claxton, Remson and Haffelfinger.
23. 1877. Canolles. Toronto: Belford Brothers.
24. 1878. Professor Pressensee. New York: Harper and Brothers.
25. 1879. Mr. Grantley's Idea. New York: Harper and Brothers.
26. 1879. Stories of the Old Dominion. New York: Harper and Brothers.
27. 1880. The Virginia Bohemians. New York: Harper and Brothers.
28. 1883. Fanchette. Boston: James R. Osgood and Company.
29. 1883. Virginia. Boston: Houghton, Mifflin and Company.
30. 1885. My Lady Pokahontas. Boston: Houghton, Mifflin and Company.
31. 1885. The Maurice Mystery. New York: D. Appleton and Company.

MAGAZINE ARTICLES

At various periods during his life Cooke contributed more or less regularly to over forty periodicals, most of which have been referred to in the text. Below is given a bibliography for four magazines. The four are chosen partly because of their literary importance and consequent present-day accessibility, but chiefly because of the fact that they received a large portion of Cooke's most carefully composed fugitive work.

The Southern Literary Messenger

Editorials and short book notices are not included in this list.

1848: November, "Avalon."
1849: January, "Eighteen Sonnets, With Notes."

1850: June, "Thomas Carlyle and his 'Latter-Day Pamphlets';" July, "The Dawning;" October, "Levon: A Memory."

1851: February and March, "Shadows of the Mountain Pine;" March, "Deliciæ Orientis;" April, "To a Portrait," "Recollections of Sully," To —— and ——;" May, "To Kossuth;" August, "Hungary;" September, "Winderhaus and the Gentleman in Black," "Indian Wars of Western Virginia;" October and November, "Shadows of the Pine Forest."

1852: January, "The Story of Good Mr. Bear;" May, "Peony: A Tale for the Times;" July, "Clouds," "My River Rhine;" August-September, "Chronicles of the Valley of Virginia;" August, "I Left the South Behind Me," "Autumn Days," "Country Notes;" December, "A Handful of Autumn Leaves."

1853: January, "Peachblossom and Ladyslipper," "Psyche looked on me with her luminous eyes;" February, "Sieur Roger;" June, "An Angling Reminiscence;" July, "News From Farnienteland;" December, "Autumn Dreams."

1854: July, "The Plover Loves the Moor;" August, "Lie Still, Poor Heart;" October-January (1855), "The Last Days of Gaston Phœbus;" December, "Invocation."

1855: May-September, "A Kingdom Mortgaged;" December, "Virginia Woods."

1856: January, "Under the Grassland Oaks," "The Winds of Childhood;" July, "Sully's Forest Days," "Virginia Girls and Gallants Four Score Years Ago."

1857: April, "Kane;" May, "In Love;" July, "Again," "The Story of Carteret," "I Often See in Happy Dreams;" November, "Cherry's Christmas Tree;" December, "Sully's Woodland Dreams."

1858: April, "Frank Lee's Engagement," "Private Opinions of Joyeuse Tristan, Gent.;" "O Fairy-Like Child of May;" May, "May Days at Rackrack Hall," "Honoria Vane;" June, "Wanderings on the Banks of the York;" September, "The Portfolio of a Rambler in Virginia;" November, "My Three Pipes," "Unpublished Mss. from the Portfolios of the Most Celebrated Authors" (reprint).

1859: January, "The Cynic;" April-December, "Greenway Court;" April, "The Song of Loronnaye;" May, "My Powhatan Pipe," "Crazy and Sane."

1860: January, 'The Moon is in the Sky;" February, "Recollections of a Contented Philosopher," "Phœbe's Wedding Night" (reprint); April, "Thomas Jefferson" (reprint); July-October, "The Knight of Espalion."
1862: February and March: "Waiting for Florella," "Day Dreaming."

Putnam's Monthly Magazine

1853: August, "Virginia: Past and Present;" December, "Minuet and Polka."
1854: March, "The Cocked Hat Gentry."
1855: May, "The Dames of Virginia."
1856: April, "How I Courted Lulu;" June, "Annie at the Corner;" July, "News from Grassland;" August, "John Randolph;" November, "The Tragedy of Hairston."
1857: June, "Greenway Court."

Harper's

1856: January, "Baby Bertie's Christmas;" April, "How I Was Discarded;" September, "Fanny and Myself," "In Memoriam."
1857: April, "The Story of a Huguenot's Sword;" July, "The Two Kates;" November, "Lost;" December, "Our Christmas at the Pines."
1858: June, "A Nest of Cavaliers;" July, "Nelly's Slipper;" August, "The Red Bracelet."
1859: January, "Only a Woman's Hair;" October, "Two Men and a Woman."
1861: January, "A Dream of the Cavaliers;" March, "A Joyous Frenchman in Virginia."
1876: June, "Virginia in the Revolution;" July, "The Writer of the Declaration."
1877: January, "A Craniologist;" April, "Old Wiley."
1878: July, "Owlet;" August, "The White Sulphur Springs."
1879: February, "The Moonshiners;" June, "Alexander Spottswood."
1880: August, "A Boating Adventure."
1881: November, "The Sumac-Gatherers."
1884: June, "Grace Sherwood, the One Virginia Witch;" December, "Toinette."

Appleton's Journal

1869: May 29, "My Wicker-Seat;" August 14, "Royalty in Miniature;" September 25, "The Horseshoe Knights;" December 4, "Washington's Wedding."

1870: January 22, "The Sword and Surveying Instruments of Washington;" July 2, "Authors and Their Work;" November 26, "A Struggle for Life."

1871: February 11, 18, "The Natural Bridge;" November 4, "Some Old Virginia Houses;" November 18, "Alexandre Dumas;" December 23, "Old Blandford Church;" December 30, "Flower of the Daisy."

1872: April 20, "Old Virginia Manners;" September 21, "The Last Hours of Barras;" October 5, "The Cotton-Mouth."

1873: February 8, "M. Thiers in His Study" (From the French of A. de Pontmartin); July 19, "Historic Houses in the Shenandoah;" August 16, "The Author of 'Swallow Barn';" September 12, "Mistletoe Hall;" December 20, "The Braddock House."

1874: January 3, "Bonny Jean;" January 24, "Stratford House;" February 7, "Miss Muhlbach and Her System;" April 4, "Gunston Hall;" May 2, "An Author's Way of Working;" June 13, "Pontmartin, the French Critic;" August 15, "Christ Church, Alexandria;" August 22, "Jefferson as a Lover;" August 29, "Cooper's Indians;" November 28, "Old St. Peter's Church;" December 5, "The Moore House, Yorktown;" December 12, "Heaving Bricks."

1875: January 9, "The Personal Character of General Lee;" March 20, "The Thursdays of Madame Charbonneau;" July 17, "Fairy Fingers: A Few Notes for My Friends the Painters;" December 11, 18, 25, "Suzanne Gervaz: A Maid of the Gévaudan" (Adapted from "Les Corbeaux du Gévaudan" by de Pontmartin).

1876: February 5, 12, "A New View of Jacques and Touchstone;" June 24, "Book-Making in Paris."

1877: August, "My Lady Mary."

1878: April, "The Wonderful Family."

1879: September, "An Hour With Thackeray."

INDEX